A FINE STATEMENT

An Irish Poets'
Anthology

EDITED BY JOHN MCDONAGH

POOLBEG

Published 2008
by Poolbeg Press Ltd
123 Grange Hill, Baldoyle
Dublin 13, Ireland
E-mail: poolbeg@poolbeg.com
www.poolbeg.com

1 3 5 7 9 10 8 6 4 2

A catalogue record for this book is available from the British Library.

ISBN 978-1-84223-368-9

Typeset by Patricia Hope in Bembo 11/15

Printed by Printed and bound by Clays Ltd, UK

Personal Acknowledgements

Sincere thanks are due to all the poets who contributed to this collection, for their patience, promptness and willingness to cooperate. Peter Fallon and Anne Duggan at The Gallery Press were extremely helpful in a variety of ways and for that I am particularly grateful. Stephen Newman of the Department of Irish at Mary Immaculate College, Limerick, provided invaluable assistance with the Irish language poems. Dr Eugene O'Brien, Head of the Department of English Language and Literature at Mary Immaculate College, was supportive of this project from the outset and genuine thanks are due to him. Heartfelt thanks also to Brian Langan at Poolbeg Press for his professionalism, enthusiasm and willingness to take on the project. Finally, thanks to my wife Trish, for, to put it simply, everything.

To John, Brigid, Patrick, Michael and Meabh.

You are my finest statements.

CONTENTS

INTRODUCTION

All the poets included in this anthology have chosen five of what they regard as their most significant poems, collected over a lifetime's work and selected without any editorial control whatsoever. The choices they have made are revealing. Signature poems, instantly recognisable works that would generally appear in most anthologies, rub shoulders with lesser known and often more recent works. Evidently, poets like to be regarded for their latest compositions as well as the works that established their reputations in the first place. Many of the poets expressed the difficulty of the task, careful that their choices reflected both their traditional and current concerns.

What is fascinating about the selection of poems chosen by the poets themselves is the extent to which the poems appear to coalesce around the autobiographical. For example, John Montague's magnificent poem "Last Court", from his 2004 collection *Drunken Sailor*, typifies this autobiographical self-analysis, blending the everyday details of a private life with a searing and touching honesty. It is narrative poetry at its best, seamlessly combining the rich rhythm of the lyric with the candour and integrity of a man facing up to the often difficult relationship he had with his brother over a number of years. The poem in many ways exemplifies not only the collection as a whole but contemporary Irish poetry in general, moving its geographical locus from the small village of Fintona in County Tyrone to Florence in Italy, via West Cork and Brooklyn. The ease of geographical movement in the poem reflects the changes wrought in the nature of Irish life in the past twenty years, with millions of return plane journeys on cheap budget airlines replacing the one-way ferry from Dun Laoghaire to Holyhead or the American wake. Europe and the wider world are a lot closer and are therefore a far greater reference point for a lot more Irish people than heretofore. Similarly, Theo Dorgan's

"Ithaca" charts a journey away from the eponymous Greek island, the home of Odysseus around whom James Joyce built his Leopold Bloom. The lesson to be learned about life, according to Dorgan, is that "the wind sweeps everything away", and he points to a future that, "free from home", offers endless possibilities. The positivity that runs through this poem is certainly indicative of this collection as a whole.

In their introduction to the influential *The Penguin Book of Contemporary Irish Poetry*, first published in 1990, editors Peter Fallon and Derek Mahon note that Irish poetry "speaks for itself in one or another of the many voices which have evolved over the years"[1] and this crucial acknowledgement in an important and popular anthology points clearly to the disparate, polyvocal and chimerical nature of a good deal of current Irish poetry up to 1990 and beyond. Ranging from Cathal Ó Searchaigh's homoerotic odes to his gay lover to Paul Durcan's laments over the crass materialism of contemporary Ireland, recent Irish poetry has been clearly marked by the notable absence of a dominant voice and an eclectic, surprising and challenging range of subject matter. Light has been shone on almost every manifestation of contemporary Irish life by poets displaying, in Louis de Paor's wonderful phrase, an "agitated intelligence"[2] in the wake of widespread social and economic changes.

What can be said with any certainty is that contemporary Irish poetry is marked by a broad range of confident voices articulating a tentative recognition of the complex nature of major shifts in the traditional markers of Irish identity. In the North, for example, the changing social and political landscape is equally reflected in the discontinuous narrative of the major poetic voices, including Seamus Heaney, Medbh McGuckian and Ciaran Carson, an uncertainty captured by the latter in "Belfast Confetti" when his self-image reflects a national questioning: "My name? Where am I coming from? Where am I going? A / fusillade of question marks"[3]. Newer voices,

---

[1] Peter Fallon and Derek Mahon (eds.), *The Penguin Book of Contemporary Irish Poetry* (Penguin, London, 1990), p. xxii.

[2] Louis de Paor, "Contemporary Poetry in Irish: 1940–2000" in Margaret Kelleher and Philip O'Leary (eds.), *The Cambridge History of Irish Literature* (Cambridge University Press, Cambridge, 2006), p. 349.

[3] Ciaran Carson, *The Irish For No* (The Gallery Press, Oldcastle, 1987), p. 31.

including Sinéad Morrissey, are emerging from this changed environment, less concerned perhaps with their political heritage than with charting a new path forward. Morrissey's five poems interestingly concern themselves with conception, birth and death, and the pressing in of one upon the other. Her images of journeys from place to place and from life to death indicate an innate restlessness, and the last words of "Found Architecture" are "ready to jump", a clear laying down of a new poetic imperative.

Ironically, the very lack of a predominant school or voice places greater pressure on critical reflections of the nature of contemporary Irish life. What can be said is that there are few if any areas of contemporary experience that are not subject to poetic inquiry. This confidence in the future, and a tacit recognition of the resonance of the past, is summed up by Micheal O'Siadhail, one of the most accomplished and accessible poets to emerge in the 1990s, in his poem "Tremolo", one of his own choices for this collection:

> Given riffs and breaks of our own,
> Given a globe of boundless jazz,
> Yet still a remembered undertone,
>
> A quivering earthy line of soul
> Crying in all diminished chords.
> Our globe still trembles on its pole

O'Siadhail's work acts as an exemplar of the nature of contemporary Irish poetry, particularly south of the border. His collections showcase a poet at home in his own, fragile sense of humanity, sensitively aware of the everyday concerns that consume so much time and refreshingly free from any sense of an over-arching theme or agenda. His poetry is that of almost instant recognition, often unadorned, eschewing complex imagery yet crafted with a sharp eye on the unity of form and subject. Contemporary life in Ireland is shown to be inescapably complex and one which offers a greater degree of intellectual and emotional honesty and freedom in a cultural climate that is in a frenzied state of flux. O'Siadhail's work points to the emergence of an Ireland that is unsure of where it is going but is in an awful hurry to get there!

It is important to point out, however, that this headlong rush into the next stage of Irish modernity is marked by a respect for the past and an acknowledgement of the crucial importance of tradition in the formation of new models of national identity. Many of the poems included in this collection are marked by what could be called a modern nostalgia, exemplified in the beautiful "Death of a Field" by Paula Meehan. She alludes to all that is lost in the process of development and the irony that one of the consequences of the economic drive towards increased prosperity is the destruction of the very environment that supports it in the first place, a clear metaphor for the problems facing the environment in the future. In many senses, her poem becomes, in itself, a footprint recording all that is being lost in the gradual spread of urbanisation across the Irish landscape. Derek Mahon's hauntingly evocative "A Garage in Co. Cork", while tracing the gradual decimation of a rural community through emigration, points to the necessity of change and he acknowledges the concurrent displacement of a sense of home, a feature of many of the poems in this collection. Again, however, this sense of homelessness is greeted with a pragmatism born out of a realisation of its temporary nature. Indeed, the last stanza of this influential poem expresses a sentiment very close to that of O'Siadhail's "Tremolo" and could be regarded as the anthem for this current generation of Irish poets:

> We might be anywhere but are in one place only,
> One of the milestones of earth-residence
> Unique in each particular, the thinly
> Peopled hinterland serenely tense –
> Not in the hope of a resplendent future
> But with a sure sense of its intrinsic nature.

In a time of huge technological advances, from iPhones to mass internet usage, contemporary poetry can occasionally reinvent itself as a repository of the past, recording an environment and a way of life as it passes and is superseded by an uncertain future. What needs to be stressed, however, is the degree to which the poets in this collection appear to embrace this change, welcoming the many advances of Irish culture and society while remaining mindful of the significance of the past. Peter Fallon's beautifully constructed poem "Gate" is an example of this remembering; the rusty gate in the middle of a field "stops nothing and points nowhere" yet its very presence acts as a reminder of the temporality of life. Once this iron gate had a clear and definitive purpose, now it is ignored by the cattle and horses who amble by. However, rather than being portrayed as a symbol of a defunct and irrelevant past, the gate becomes symbolic of all gates, metaphors for entering a bright future. Fallon notes a brief hesitation, then a grasping of unknown opportunities:

Then you pause. And open it. And enter.

Kerry Hardie's poignant long poem "Exiles" taps into this meshing of tradition and change when she exhorts the importance of recollection in a time of transformation: "To remember, in a time of forgetting". Indeed, this could be the mantra of many of the poems in this anthology, a desire to cling to some perceived certainties in a period of rapid and irrevocable change. Hardie's poem is an evocation of the complexities of ageing and the almost inevitable nostalgia that accompanies the passing of a generation. Seamus Heaney's wonderfully titled "A Sofa in the Forties" brings the reader back to a simpler, less technologically driven era of play when a humble sofa packed with children could be transformed into anything from a ghost train plummeting into the unspeakable darkness to the Wild West pioneers establishing the frontiers of the fledgling United States. The poet and his siblings are crammed onto a rickety leatherette couch, their imaginations in overdrive as they convert the uncomfortable seat into a train hurtling towards an unknown destination. The poem is a celebration of the transformative power of the imagination, and a shining example of the humour that Heaney so often injects into his work.

However, it is again essential to stress that neither Hardie nor Heaney are engaging in some mawkish sentimentality over *la temps perdue* but rather are acknowledging where they have come from and the significance of these origins in the attempted understanding of the present. Again, this celebration of personal origins emerges in the tender images in Bernard O'Donoghue's "*Ter Conatus*" where he captures the awkward yet exquisite tenderness between a brother and sister running a farm together for sixty years until she loses her battle with cancer. As with all of O'Donoghue's work, the poem is beautifully weighted and delicately constructed, the siblings emblematic of a passing era of politeness and unspoken loyalties. The brashness of the contemporary is noticeably absent in this portrayal of a relationship founded on the unspoken. This pragmatism runs throughout the poems selected here and is indicative of the confidence that exudes from poets writing in a country emerging into what many would regard as a brave new world. Medbh McGuckian's "Viewing Neptune Through a Glass Telescope" is another example of the sensitivity of perspective noticeable in so many poems in this collection. From her place on this "coloured earth" she can see "nothing but the world as a whole", this idea of looking at the self from both an outward- and inward-looking perspective echoing the internationalism of contemporary Irish poetry yet clinging tenaciously to a sense of what it means to be Irish.

The rationales offered by the poets for their choices are a fascinating and unique feature of this anthology. Most of the poets remarked that this was the first occasion when they had been asked to select their own poems and many expressed great difficulty in selecting just five. These notes are revealing. Most are tinged with uncertainty, a nagging feeling that the selection of poems could be different at any given time. Clearly what critics consider to be "important" signature poems are regarded as more prosaic writings by what Derek Mahon playfully calls "the perpetrator". Indeed, these signature poems, which established the reputations of many of the poets, are often ignored or regarded as weary millstones that overshadow other, more favoured, works. John Montague somewhat light-heartedly refers to two of his poems currently on the Leaving Certificate syllabus "breaking young hearts in the Republic", a self-critical honesty that characterises many of the contributions. It would appear that what critics value in a poem can often be radically different from what the poet intended. Eavan Boland's rationale typifies the honesty and candour behind the choices made in this collection. Far from decamping to imaginary ivory towers, the poets here want to engage with the world and expose themselves as fragile, open selves, as much tossed and buffeted in this turbulent world as anybody else:

> "I think most poets stay connected to poems they've written for more or less the same reason: that they retain some of the hopes and intensities with which they started out. No other consistency – not subject matter, nor style, nor concept – matters as much to me. When I read these poems I remember some of those original feelings. Which is why I chose them."

The key to the choices would appear to be the attempt to trace a development, a progression towards a receding goal. Clearly poetry is a life-long, organic process, the themes diverging and recurring and the style of each poet maturing as lives become more complicated, interests change and perspectives shift. The most recent poems are clearly very important to poets, indicative of the chimerical nature of the muse. Many of the poets included unpublished poems, new works that reflect current concerns and it is interesting to trace the changes in the works. Overall, the impression created by the responses was that this was a surprisingly difficult exercise, suggesting that the process of selection is as difficult for a poet as it is for a prospective anthologist.

In the Republic, the economic boom of the 1990s continued to make waves into the 2000s, heralding unparalleled prosperity, increased urbanisation and large-scale immigration, a triumvirate destined to place pressure on accepted models of a collective national perspective. These changes are not ignored by the poetry being written in contemporary Ireland. For its continued social and intellectual relevance, it is essential that poetry reflects on more than the aesthetic, and this is clearly noticeable in this collection. For example, the holocaust and its resonance in modern European history is an event that echoes through a surprising number of the chosen poems, again highlighting the influence of Europe on contemporary Ireland. Many of these poems exude what Patrick Kavanagh referred to as a national outward-looking insularity, a mischievous oxymoron that acknowledges the constant importance of events outside Ireland on the development of the native culture. Michael Longley's achingly evocative "Ghetto" traces a journey from a ghetto to the concentration camp, often seen through the eyes of children, whose "last belonging is a list of belongings". His often unsentimental portrayal of the detail of a shattered life, from "broken hobby-horses" to "silent toys", brings the abstract notion of genocide to its full brutal, human manifestation. As with Montague, Longley moves easily both chronologically and geographically, paralleling the Northern Ireland troubles with the Trojan Wars in poems that are instinctively focused on the individual experience of grief. It is from these experiences that Longley allows the reader to reflect on poems suffused with a natural empathy for the lone voice of the single human being.

What is immediately noticeable about the choices made by the poets is the number of long poems that they have chosen. Irish poetry has a long connection to the epic form and indeed many of the most significant poems in the development of contemporary poetry have been variations on the epic. Patrick Kavanagh's 1942 masterpiece, *The Great Hunger*, was over 700 lines long and is a hugely significant poem in the emergence of what could be termed the modern epic. It would appear that an Irish poet has to earn their stripes by tackling the long poem, a work driven by a narrative and derived from a well-established story-telling tradition. The long poem clearly allows the poet room to explore an idea in depth and to range over both time and space. The Haiku is emerging in contemporary Ireland as a popular poetic form, but the long poem, with a central heroic figure enduring all that life throws at them, is a form that most Irish poets appear happy to utilise. Equally, on a more pragmatic level, perhaps the fact that the poets were encouraged to include whatever poems they wished facilitated the airing of certain long poems that normally would not feature in anthologies.

Ciaran Carson epitomises this contemporary reworking of the epic in many of his poems. "Dresden", for example, is a long poem that trawls through the tragicomic lives of twins Horse and Mule Boyle. Because of its length and Carson's gift for astute, observational storytelling, their broken lives become metaphorical of the Northern troubles, shattered by poverty and alcoholism against a violent and turbulent political backdrop. The destruction of millions of delicate porcelain figures during the RAF bombing of Dresden, where Horse acted as a rear-gunner, again emphasises the connectedness of humanity in the face of apparently irreconcilable differences. Many years later, as Horse reflects on the destruction, he drops his favourite porcelain figure, a milkmaid, her broken outstretched hand retrieved and stored in an old biscuit tin. Like all good poets, Carson is recording a life that is vanishing and, in many cases, a life that has disappeared altogether.

So what do contemporary Irish poets have to say about our modern state? What strands can be detected connecting twenty-first-century Ireland with perceptions of its past, and indeed what tentative images of the present can be seen to emerge? The poems in this collection portray an Ireland coming to terms with change – political, social and cultural. Iconic markers of Irish identity, such as emigration, Catholicism and ruralism are under pressure from new forces, such as immigration, increased wealth, secularisation and a rapid urbanisation. Those who are being left behind in all this flux find a voice in the poems here. What is critically important about poetry, then, is its continuous ability to unsettle and undermine perceived certainties. Equally, what has continually maintained poetry's vitality and cultural importance is its resistance to the contemporary culture, articulating the alternative voices that speak of new and exciting aspects of modernity. In the poem "Service", in Brendan Kennelly's brilliant 1991 epic *The Book of Judas*, the eponymous Iscariot laconically notes that "The best way to serve the age is to betray it"[4] and it is precisely this form of subversion that gives so much contemporary Irish poetry its social, cultural, political and literary relevance. This reworking of the concept of betrayal is based largely on a desire to resist a casual labelling in which the complexities of both individuals and ideologies are glossed over, and in the preface to *The Book of Judas* Kennelly warns of the dangers of reductionism inherent in all forms of social and cultural classification.

---

[4] Brendan Kennelly, *The Book of Judas* (Bloodaxe Books, Newcastle, 1991), p. 17.

Contemporary Irish poetry is marked by this note of resistance. Michael Hartnett brilliantly described poetry's ability to surprise at the end of his poem "For My God-daughter, B.A.H.":

> for there is an Ireland, where
> trees suddenly fly away
> and leave their pigeons, baffled,
> standing in the air.[5]

One of the constant "flying trees" of the past forty years has been Paul Durcan, a serial demythologiser, a self-demythologiser and a relentless commentator on the rolling maul that is Irish identity. Durcan's long poetic career has been marked by an often unnerving emotional honesty and a recurring desire to undermine the pomposity of an Ireland struggling under the weight of inherited inconsistencies. Since his earliest solo collection, *O Westport in the Light of Asia Minor* in 1975, Durcan has satirised and caricatured Irish life like no other contemporary poet. His often incongruous narratives, borrowing heavily from surrealism, juxtapose the absurd and the normal. His stinging attacks on the new Irish bourgeoisie is only matched by his contempt for the pretensions of literary and cultural society, making him the natural contemporary successor of Patrick Kavanagh. Where Kavanagh railed against what he perceived to be the literary mediocrity of 1950s Dublin in "The Paddiad" – "The boys go wild and toast the Joker / The master of the mediocre"[6] – Durcan has been an early critical observer of the emergence of what is commonly known as the Celtic Tiger. The very preposterousness of many of his poem titles, including "Margaret Thatcher Joins the IRA", "Irish Hierarchy Bans Colour Photography" and "Archbishop of Kerry to have Abortion" points to his delight in upsetting traditional perspectives and inverting the perceived ideologies at work in Irish society.

---

[5] Michael Hartnett, *Poems to Younger Women* (The Gallery Press, Oldcastle, 1989), p. 33.
[6] Peter Kavanagh (ed.), *Patrick Kavanagh – Complete Poems* (The Goldsmith Press, Newbridge, 1972), p. 213.

Durcan's work also illustrates the importance of the European dimension in the development of contemporary Irish poetry, a dimension that is very apparent in many of the poems in this collection. His poems are indicative of a generation of poets, particularly south of the border, no longer obsessed with the Anglo-Irish dimension but determined to look further afield for resonances of common identity. In the hilariously titled "Diarrhoea Attack at Party Headquarters in Leningrad" Durcan muses over the randomness of fate as he recovers from a bout of bowel trouble on a trip to Leningrad:

> – My ignominy – not anybody else's ignominy – and that night
> Over cups of tea we discussed the war in Afghanistan,
> Agreeing that realistically it appeared an insoluble problem,
> Yet hoping against hope that somehow it would be solved
> And that – as you put it, Slava – "Russian boys come home."
> There is nothing necessarily ignominious about anything.

The brilliant last line of this poem (one of his choices) is an exemplar of the acute ability of the seemingly comic and banal to speak a universal truth. Durcan's bout of diarrhoea occurs in the Communist Party Headquarters in Leningrad, the emotional heartland of one of the great Western counter-meta-narratives of the second half of the twentieth century, namely Red Russia. Now here is a meta-narrative with a life outside third-level seminar rooms and PhD theses! Vladimir Lenin, in all his portrayed glory, looks down on the stricken poet, empathising with his discomfort and somehow reaching out over the Grand Hall of the People to the buckled poet staggering towards his waiting car. Durcan's diarrhoea initiates a conversation between him and his interpreter, Slava, in which the reality of the loss of human life in the name of bankrupt ideologies becomes their emotional bond, cemented by healing cups of communal tea. The real ignominy of life is death and it often takes a moment of apparent absurdity, brilliantly recounted by Durcan, to remind us that we take so much for granted. Here, arguably, is the most effective methodology of the postmodern Irish poet, juxtaposing the absurd and the ridiculous with the profound and the philosophical in such a way that whatever truth the artist is attempting to articulate emerges in the most surprising ways. Brendan Kennelly is right when he states that real identity lurks in the nooks and crannies of self and it is in the absurd that the postmodern finds its most effective social and cultural critique. There are no sacred cows in the poems of Paul Durcan. Indeed, his work is a veritable Halal abattoir in which pretensions, hypocrisies, posers and chancers have a razor-sharp blade traced across their throats, bleeding forth their duplicity, pretence and double-standards. Durcan does this with a black humour and lightness of touch that mark him out as one of the most effective and insightful social critics this country has produced.

Another poet who would also appears to break with perceived markers of Irish identity is Cathal Ó Searchaigh. A gay Buddhist Irish- language poet and playwright living at the foot of Mount Errigal in County Donegal, Ó Searchaigh occupies many of the spaces that stand in opposition to the traditionally dominant markers of Irish identity. However, he is a complex poet, combining angry poetry railing against the discrimination meted out to those in Ireland who do not conform to the orthodoxies with a Kavanaghesque delight expressed in poems celebrating the simple and rugged beauty of the Donegal countryside. Ó Searchaigh writes of his Iraqi lover Yusuf and the difficulties faced by him since the beginning of the latest war to hit that country. His homo-erotic poems are explicit, relishing in a sensuality that for many years rarely found explicit expression in Irish literature. In a poem entitled "Laoi Chumainn", for example (translated by Frank Sewell and entitled "Serenade"), Ó Searchaigh parodies the Red Branch heroes of Lady Gregory when he portrays his lover in terms of a rampant Celtic warrior:

> So, tonight, if there's a war to wage, my love,
> let it be here among these pillows.
> Raise your shield and hurl your lance,
>   aim your sword
> exactly. Get that war-cry off your chest.
> And I will be here, all eyes

at the manhood
moving in you, my passionate one, until you come
to meet me through sheets and pillows.[7]

While not quite at the level of Myles na gCopaleen's legendary Celtic
parodies, Ó Searchaigh's evocation of a warrior complete with shield, lance and
sword allows an army of *double-entendres* a freeplay of delicious irony,
underscoring the homo-erotic undertones of a good deal of traditional Irish
Celtic literature and mythology. However, Ó Searchaigh is well aware of the slow
change of pace in the public's perception of gay love when he notes that
"tomorrow, we'll pay for being flesh and blood", an acknowledgement that old
prejudices are often much slower to follow economic and social changes. His
homoerotic poems celebrating the sexual union between him and another man
are unambiguously explicit, allowing the love that dare not speak its name a clear
expression in the context of a society far more at ease with competing models
of sexual orientation, recognised by the decriminalisation of homosexuality in
the Republic in the early 1990s. Ó Searchaigh's poetry is a strong indication that
the Catholic/heterosexual axis of Irish identity, enshrined in the 1937
constitution, is no longer the only model of identity in town.

Equally, Ó Searchaigh's promotion of the Irish language is an important
marker of the re-emergence of the national language as a serious player in the
development of contemporary Irish poetry. While translation studies shed
revealing and challenging light on the nature of the development of
contemporary Irish poetry, an overview of this progression cannot ignore the
vitality and range of poetry written in the Irish language. Throughout the 1990s,
many Irish language poets, including Michael Hartnett (1941–99), Michael Davitt
(1950–2005) and Nuala Ní Dhomhnaill (b.1952), have written poetry in Irish that
is every bit as socially and culturally challenging as its English-language
counterparts. This collection is also marked by a high concentration of poems
originally written in Irish but translated into English. The principal difficulty
facing Irish language poetry is obviously the thorny issue of translation into

---

[7] Cathal Ó Searchaigh, *An Bealach 'na Bhaile* (Cló Iar-Chonnachta Teo, Conamara, 1991), p. 5.

English, and many prominent contemporary poets have used the kind offices of fellow poets to bring their Irish language poetry to an English-speaking audience.

A fascinating example occurs in this collection with Paul Muldoon's translation of Nuala Ní Dhomhnaill's "An Crann". Muldoon entitles the poem "As for the Quince", despite the fact that the literal translation of Ní Dhomhnaill's title should be "The Tree". The marital strife that is paralleled by the fate of the tree is full of ironic humour in both poems, but Muldoon goes further by adding an entire line that does not appear in the original. His addition of "*et cetera et cetera*" is a telling and humourous moment in the poem, the cause of the tiff reduced to an inconsequential shibboleth. Muldoon's poem should rightly be called a version rather than a translation and this is a recurring feature of much Irish language poetry that is translated into English. A classic example of this linguistic exchange can be found in the work of Michael Hartnett, who famously turned his back on English in 1974, only to return triumphantly a decade later with his *Inchicore Haiku*, one of which beautifully summed up his linguistic dilemma:

> My English dam bursts
> And out stroll all my bastards
> Irish shakes its head[8]

Rita Ann Higgins has long been one of the most astute and sharp observers of the changes that have come about in Irish society over the last twenty years. She has charted the gradual emergence of what she perceives to be an uncaring society turning its back on the marginalised, prepared to accept collateral casualties in its drive for more and more economic success. With Ireland's rapid economic growth of the past fifteen years has come an inevitable widening of the chasm between those who have benefited from years of sustained economic growth and those whose poverty and exclusion is merely exacerbated by the rising tide of prosperity. There are no off-limits with Higgins, from her own personal struggles with addiction to subjects that are tragic in the extreme but

---

[8] Michael Hartnett, *Inchicore Haiku* (Raven Arts Press, Dublin, 1985), p. 9.

which flicker in and out of public consciousness. In an unpublished poem, entitled "The Immortals", she touchingly and sardonically portrays the brief lives of what have euphemistically become known in contemporary Irish parlance as "boy racers", young men driving usually old but modified cars up and down the highways and byways of Ireland. Higgins portrays the minutiae of a sub-culture, from the baseball caps to Recaro bucket seats, from gaudy colours to functionless accessories. She captures a culture in which social and economic powerlessness is converted into God-like supremacy behind the wheel of a modified car. The conversion of the roads of rural Ireland from John Hinde images of cattle-herding to sites of apparently relentless fatalities is epitomised with the mention of Spiddal, the gateway to Connemara and the spiritual home of the Irish *Gaeltacht*:

> quicken on the Spiddal road
> in Barbie Pink souped-ups
> or roulette red Honda Civics.
> With few fault lines or face lifts to rev up about
> only an unwritten come hither of thrills
> with screeching propositions and no full stops –
> if you are willing to ride the ride.

The juxtaposition of the iconic fields of Connemara with the burning rubber of the red Honda Civic provides the poem with one of its central dynamics and Higgins is unafraid of dealing with the inevitable tragedies that such activities entail:

> On headstones made from Italian marble
> they become "our loving son Keith"
> "our beloved son Jonathan", etcetera etcetera.
> On the Spiddal road
> itching to pass out the light
> they become Zeus, Eros, Vulcan, Somnus.[9]

---

[9] Rita Ann Higgins, unpublished poem, 2007.

Again, the last line of this poem is beautifully weighted. The fatalistic journey in the car transforms the boy racer into believing his infallibility, from the God of Gods (Zeus) to the eternal sleep of the grave (Somnus). No penalty points or speed cameras are going to have the slightest effect on this journey because this transformation is intoxicating. The freedom offered by the car and the road to a boy marginalised from many avenues of social and cultural advancement cannot be replaced. The split second journey from Zeus to Somnus is destined to be eternally played out on boreens from Malin Head to Mizen. Again, as in the poems of Paul Durcan, Higgins deals with real social problems, merging the aesthetic with the real in poems of often shocking clarity.

This feature of contemporary Irish poetry – namely the regular intrusion of subjects normally associated with other genres – certainly adds a great deal of bite to the current crop of poets unafraid to deal not only with their most personal experiences, from addiction to depression, but also with contemporary social issues. These concerns may date these poems somewhat as the latest cultural concerns are forgotten and replaced by new ones, but they also give contemporary Irish poetry a far greater handle on the *zeitgeist* than in previous eras. Perhaps Adrian Mitchell's often-quoted maxim that most people ignore poetry because poetry ignores most people is one that cannot be applied either to the work of Rita Ann Higgins or to a good proportion of poets writing in Ireland today. Higgins's Ireland is a place of social and cultural disillusionment, populated by a tranche of individuals who have, unwittingly and otherwise, missed the bus of the economic boom. Her satirical and lacerating critiques of the pretensions of what would commonly be known as "the chattering classes" are laced with a biting humour and her harassed characters act as a wonderful counter-balance to a culture that prides itself on an unwavering confidence. She unflinchingly deals with the darker side of life in the Republic, ranging from the epidemic of suicide to the unrelenting death tolls in road accidents and her poetry is a barometer of the many casualties of Ireland's social and cultural development. Indeed, the witty and surreal cover to her 2001 collection, *An Awful Racket,* featured the late Pope John Paul II preaching to a flock of penguins on an iceberg, indicative of the drift away from traditional authority that is so characteristic of contemporary Ireland.

While many of the poems reflect the changes wrought in Irish society in the last twenty years or so, it is interesting to note the recurrence of more familiar concerns. One recurring theme is the centrality of family in the formation of a sense of identity. Grand-parents, parents, partners, husbands, wives, brothers, sisters, children and grandchildren (even the unborn!) appear throughout the collection, acting as a type of correlative by which the poet begins to conceive of a sense of self. Pat Boran's "Children" emphasises the crucial formative role of childhood, where events from the past, often half-remembered, return to play a crucial role in adulthood. He captures this in a delicate image:

> We leave their fingerprints
> On everything we touch.

The family, be it that one we emerge from or the one that we stumble into, is the crucible that contains the people who, more than any others, become the yardsticks by which we judge our own lives. The poems resonate with conflicts, moments of tenderness and seminal relationships, often coalescing around parents and children. In her note, Medbh McGuckian honestly observes that "it is hard to be too careful in protecting the creative self from the suffering self" and this is a caveat that could be applied to many of the poems in this collection. Indeed, Nuala Ni Dhomhnaill's poem "Máthair" ("Mother") portrays an unsentimental, harsh and cold image of motherhood. The mother figure, however metaphorical, is one whose influence has to be internalised and overcome. The stereotype of the doting Irish mammy is dealt a fatal blow with images of constant berating and belittling, even to the point of a disregard for life itself. While Ní Dhomhnaill's poem could be read as a metaphor for the emergence of the artistic soul against hostile forces, the fact that the metaphor is that of a mother is noteworthy in itself.

In this collection, the predominance of poems that delve into family relationships, relationship breakdown and psychological traumas clearly point to the cathartic nature of poetry writing, each poem performing a mini-exorcism for the poet. Eavan Boland's "Love", for example, is a poignant reminiscing on a long marriage, a blazing and all-consuming love gradually tailing off into familiarity yet retaining the delicious intensity and desire of its initial beginning. She wonders if that birthplace can ever be revisited, but her "words are shadows" and hopes fade into the falling snow. However, it would be unfair to portray an unremittingly bleak picture of the past in this collection, and it is noteworthy that almost all of the contributors include poems of great warmth and hope. The family unit, diffracted and remodelled, emerges from these poems as a fragile yet resolute entity that we all have to come to terms with at some stage in our lives. These poems chart a path and explore histories from which lessons can indeed be learned.

In this anthology, contemporary life in Ireland is shown to be what it is: something that cannot be grasped in its totality but which offers a greater degree of intellectual and emotional freedom in a cultural climate that is in a frenzied state of change. The baby is in no danger of being thrown out with the bathwater, however, as the past and its inherent traditions are inextricably bound up with perceptions of the present. Contemporary Irish poetry is undoubtedly in rude health, populated by poets secure in their own identities and fully prepared to engage, on any level, with whatever comes into their sights. This collection, which includes many of the most important poets of the last fifty years, clearly shows that poetry matters in contemporary Ireland and that those entrusted with its legacy are determined and immensely qualified to maintain it. The last lines of John Montague's "Last Court" could be the anthem for this latest generation of poets:

> I assert the right of love to choose,
> from whatever race, or place. And of verse
> to allay, to heal, our tribal curse, that narrowness.

John McDonagh
August 2008

EAVAN BOLAND

These poems don't have too much in common in the way of subject matter or even style. They come from different books. They come from different times in my life.

I wrote "The Emigrant Irish" on a dining-room table, looking out at a garden in spring when my children were small: it tries to describe a real displacement. I wrote "Atlantis: A Lost Sonnet" more than twenty years later, and a continent away in California. It also writes about displacement, but this time a legendary one.

I wrote "Love" and "A Woman Painted on a Leaf" in the same year, and published them in the same book, *In a Time of Violence*, in 1994. But there the similarities end. The poems are different in every way. "How the Dance Came to the City" was published in a more recent book. It has the quirky feature that it took me longest to write.

All this makes it sound as if the principle of selection was completely random. But it wasn't. I think most poets stay connected to poems they've written for more or less the same reason: that they retain some of the hopes and intensities with which they started out. No other consistency – not subject matter, nor style, nor concept – matters as much to me. When I read these poems I remember some of those original feelings. Which is why I chose them.

Atlantis – A Lost Sonnet

How on earth did it happen, I used to wonder
that a whole city – arches, pillars, colonnades,
not to mention vehicles and animals – had all
one fine day gone under?

I mean, I said to myself, the world was small then.
Surely a great city must have been missed?
I miss our old city –

white pepper, white pudding, you and I meeting
under fanlights and low skies to go home in it. Maybe
what really happened is

this: the old fable-makers searched hard for a word
to convey that what is gone is gone forever and
never found it. And so, in the best traditions of

where we come from, they gave their sorrow a name
and drowned it.

A Woman Painted on a Leaf

I found it among curios and silver,
in the pureness of wintry light.

A woman painted on a leaf.

Fine lines drawn on a veined surface
in a hand-made frame.

This is not my face. Neither did I draw it.

A leaf falls in a garden.
The moon cools its aftermath of sap.
The pith of summer dries out in starlight.

A woman is inscribed there.

This is not death. It is the terrible
suspension of life.

I want a poem
I can grow old in. I want a poem I can die in.

I want to take
this dried-out face,
as you take a starling from behind iron,
and return it to its element of air, of ending –

so that autumn
which was once
the hard look of stars,
the frown on a gardener's face,
a gradual bronzing of the distance,

will be,
from now on,
a crisp tinder underfoot. Cheekbones. Eyes. Will be
a mouth crying out. Let me.

Let me die.

How the Dance Came to the City

It came with the osprey, the cormorants, the air
at the edge of the storm, on the same route as
the blight and with the nightly sweats that said fever.

It came with the scarlet tunics and rowel-spurs,
with the epaulettes and their poisonous drizzle of gold,
with the boots, the gloves, the whips, the flash of the cuirasses.

It came with a sail riding the empire-blue haze
of the horizon growing closer, gaining and then
it was there: the whole creaking orchestra of salt and canvas.

And here is the cargo, deep in the hold of the ship,
stored with the coiled ropes and crated spice and coal,
the lumber and boredom of arrival, underneath

timbers shifting and clicking from the turnaround
of the tides locked at the mouth of Dublin Bay, is
the two-step, the quick step, the whirl, the slow return.

Tonight in rooms where skirts appear steeped in tea
when they are only deep in shadow and where heat
collects at the waist, the wrist, is wet at the base of the neck,

the secrets of the dark will be the truths of the body
a young girl feels and hides even from herself as she lets fall
satin from her thighs to her ankles, as she lets herself think

how it started, just where: with the minuet, the quadrille,
the chandeliers glinting, the noise wild silk makes and
her face flushed and wide-eyed in the mirror of his sword.

The Emigrant Irish

Like oil lamps we put them out the back,

of our houses, of our minds. We had lights
better than, newer than and then

a time came, this time and now
we need them. Their dread, makeshift example.

They would have thrived on our necessities.
What they survived we could not even live.
By their lights now it is time to
imagine how they stood there, what they stood with,
that their possessions may become our power.

Cardboard. Iron. Their hardships parcelled in them.
Patience. Fortitude. Long-suffering
in the bruise-coloured dusk of the New World.

And all the old songs. And nothing to lose.

Love

Dark falls on this mid-western town
where we once lived when myths collided.
Dusk has hidden the bridge in the river
which slides and deepens to become the water
the hero crossed on his way to hell.

Not far from here is our old apartment.
We had a kitchen and an Amish table.
We had a view. And we discovered there
love had the feather and muscle of wings
and had come to live with us,
a brother of fire and air.

We had two infant children one of whom
was touched by death in this town
and spared: and when the hero
was hailed by his comrades in hell
their mouths opened and their voices failed and
there is no knowing what they would have asked
about a life they had shared and lost.

I am your wife.
It was years ago.
Our child is healed. We love each other still.
Across our day-to-day and ordinary distances
we speak plainly. We hear each other clearly.

And yet I want to return to you
on the bridge of the Iowa river as you were,
with snow on the shoulders of your coat
and a car passing with its headlights on:

I see you as a hero in a text –
the image blazing and the edges gilded –
and I long to cry out the epic question
my dear companion:
Will we ever live so intensely again?
Will love come to us again and be
so formidable at rest it offered us ascension
even to look at him?

But the words are shadows and you cannot hear me.
You walk away and I cannot follow.

PAT BORAN

On another day I'm sure my choice of five poems to represent my work in this anthology would have been different. Though they are largely finished by the time they first see print, and therefore have to fend for themselves, I confess I worry about how the present selection will stand up in the illustrious company this anthology provides.

Even so, certain features appear common to the poems that have made this on-one-minute / off-it-the-next list over the past week or so (a week being quite enough time for such self-regarding deliberations). For me, poems usually begin from a musical impulse (a phrase, or line, or sudden run of lines, if I'm really lucky). The subject matter is often "discovered". Perhaps because of this I'm drawn to those poems that turn out to have something to say about the world, as well as, perhaps, a memorable way of saying it. For a poem to lodge long-term in memory, let alone in the heart, it needs to have at least something of both: inner music and outward connection.

"Children" and "Waving" are largely "fact" poems, or poems in which the aggregation of factual statements seemed to offer a new way of negotiating with meaning. Perhaps they provided a necessary distraction . . .

"Seven Unpopular Things to Say About Blood" is, I suppose, a kind of stumbling, awkward love poem. (What other kind is there?) Facts here are not the solution but the problem.

"Machines" is a report from the troubled centre of contemporary life, in this case a hostile urban environment, though the subject, I realise, emerges in a good deal of my writing no matter where it is set. Perhaps growing up on a small-town Main Street, with the countryside at my back door, has predisposed me to a weighing-up of such pros and (all mod) cons.

In many of my poems there is an amount of borrowing from "popular science" (some slight evidence in this selection), partly because the subject nudges my imagination, but also because it reminds and allows me to test the scale of my understanding, and concerns, and importance; at once to cool my fervour and stiffen my resolve. Science provides a kind of zoom focus between the microscopic and the astronomic, somewhere between which inhospitable poles language vibrates and, by times, appears to animate.

Finally, I include here "The Washing of Feet" because it is a poem that gives me pleasure to speak out loud. Being as close as I come to song (and I regret now too late that I have chosen no poem in a "received form" here), it links me back to my first experience of poetry as an aural rather than a literary event.

After the business/busyness of the other poems, this final offering makes (not too noisily, I hope) a plea for calm, for stillness, and for listening: three prerequisites for the making – and the appreciation – of so many things, poems among them, that one might wish to survive a life of distraction and second thoughts.

Children

Children in ill-fitting uniforms
drive adults to school, and children
argue the cost of tobacco
in the Newsagent's nearby.

You must have noticed them.

And in the mornings they rise to slaughter pigs,
cook breakfast, solve crosswords at the office . . .
Or they send tiny adults into minefields,
barefoot, with pictures
of Khomeini around their necks,
their old toes searching the sand
for death.

And children queue for Bingo
on Ormond Quay, on Mary Street,
and douse their leaking take-aways with vinegar.

And children talk and smoke incessantly
in Eastern Health Board waiting rooms,
always moving one seat to the right,
someone's parents squabbling over trinkets
on the worn linoleum.

And it is always children
who will swear for their tobacco – children
with beards and varicose veins –
and children, dressed as policemen,
who pull their first corpses from the river.

And who is it who makes love in the dark
or in the light, who haunts
and who does all our dying for us,
if not children?

We leave their fingerprints
on everything we touch.

Waving

As a child I waved to people I didn't know.
I waved from passing cars, school buses,
second floor windows, or from the street
to secretaries trapped in offices above.
When policemen motioned my father on
past the scene of the crime or an army checkpoint,
I waved back from the back seat. I loved to wave.
I saw the world disappear into a funnel
of perspective, like the reflection in a bath
sucked into a single point when the water drains.
I waved at things that vanished into points.
I waved to say, "I see you: can you see me?"

I loved "the notion of an ocean" that could wave,
of a sea that rose up to see the onlooker
standing on the beach. And, though the sea
came towards the beach, it was a different sea
when it arrived; the onlooker too had changed.
They disappeared, both of them, into points in time.
So that was why they waved to one another.
On the beach I waved until my arms hurt.

My mother waved her hair sometimes. This,
I know, seems to be something else.
But when she came up the street, bright and radiant,
her white hair like a jewel-cap on her head,
it was a signal I could not fail to answer.

I waved and she approached me, smiling shyly.
Sometimes someone walking beside her might
wave back, wondering where they knew me from.

Hands itched in pockets, muscles twitched
when I waved. "There's someone who sees me!"
But in general people took no risk with strangers,
and when they saw who I was – or wasn't –
seemed relieved, saved from terrible disgrace.

Now it turns out that light itself is a wave
(as well as a point, or points), so though for me
the waving is done, it's really just beginning.
Whole humans – arms, legs, backs and bellies –
are waving away, flickering on and off,
in and out of time and space;
pushing through the streets with their heads down,
smiling up at office windows,
lying in gutters with their kneecaps broken
and their hopes dashed; driving, loving,
hiding, growing old, but always waving,
waving as if to say: "Can you see me?
I can see you. Still . . . still . . . still . . ."

Seven Unpopular Things to Say about Blood

1
Our mothers bled, and bleed,
and our enemies,
and our enemies' mothers.

2
It rushes to the finest
nick, romances the blade.

3
It dreams
the primary dream of liquids:
to sleep, horizontally.

4
It is in the surgeon's heart,
the executioner's brain.

5
Vampires and journalists
are excited by it; poets
faint on sight.

6
I knew it better as a child,
kept scabs, like ladybirds, in jars.

7
Blood: now mine would be with yours
until the moon breaks orbit
and the nights run cold.

Machines

One night in York Street
almost ten years back – so much
drink and junk around the place

it was hard to say
just who was us, or them – one night
as I lay down to sleep on my own

cold slab of light, it started up:
below in the street, a car alarm
wielding its terrible, surgical blade

of sound. Across the way,
the College of Surgeons grinned in the night
like a skull, like a stack of skulls,

but it was hard not to cheer
when someone from a few doors up
suddenly appeared. A yard brush

like a weapon in his hands, he climbed
onto the gleaming bonnet where he stood
and began to swing,

first with aim and intent, so that
one by one the front lights went in, then
the indicators, windscreen wipers, the windscreen itself . . .

and then like some half-man, half-thing
swung, swung, swung, swung,
swung till his muscles must have ached,

till the mangled brush tumbled from his grip
and he stopped, turned, looked up at us and roared
as if his spirit could no longer be contained

by the silence, by the darkness,

by the slow-motion tragedy of
so much of Dublin back in those
and still in these dehumanising days.

The Washing of Feet

It's the simplest form of healing:
late at night,
the washing of feet.

When the light called sky
is an absence,
when the traffic's asleep;

when song
is a physical thing
needing physical shape

but you're just so worn out
facing darkness again
and those brave

tulips and roses
in Merrion Square
have long since turned in

to the dark, cottony
breath that simmers
inside of them.

When the world
is a cave, is a dungeon,
when the angels retreat,

return to this tiny
pacific ocean,
to the washing of feet.

CIARAN CARSON

"The Bomb Disposal" from *The New Estate*: From time to time in Belfast in the early 1970s, when I wrote this poem, getting from A to B could be quite complicated, and was to remain thus for many years. "Incidents" occurred at regular sporadic intervals, with their consequence of road blocks and diversions. You learned to expect the unexpected. Nevertheless there were times when you found yourself in unfamiliar territory, or saw familiar territory from a new angle. The city was a puzzle, a device to be defused.

What is our understanding of a city? How does one map any landscape? At the back of my mind was Jorge Luis Borges' prose piece "On Exactitude in Science", which is purportedly from a seventeenth-century text: "In that Empire, the Art of Cartography had attained such Perfection that the map of a single Province occupied the entirety of a City, and the map of the Empire, the entirety of a Province. In time, those Unconscionable Maps no longer satisfied, and the Cartographers' Guilds struck a Map of the Empire whose size was that of the Empire, and which coincided point for point with it." The Empire and the map end up in ruins and tatters.

"The Bomb Disposal" seems to be a precursor to my poem "Belfast Confetti", and I thought it appropriate to include it here instead of that much anthologised piece.

"Dresden" from *The Irish for No*: When I wrote this poem in about 1985 I had not been to Dresden. I was invited to read there shortly after the Berlin Wall came down. The city was still being rebuilt after the fire-bombing of 1945. I was struck especially by the ruins of the once-magnificent Frauenkirche, whose blackened stones had been laid out in neat numbered rows as a giant three-dimensional jigsaw puzzle. The church was finally rebuilt and reconsecrated in October 2005.

That model of deconstruction and reconstruction might apply to the poem itself. The narrative is a hotchpotch of personal memories, encounters, anecdotes, slightly fictionalised, or taking place in the sometimes arbitrary borderland between truth and fiction. In this it resembles the methods of some traditional storytellers. I'm thinking in particular of the late John Campbell of Mullaghbawn, whose stories operated to a general template into which various digressions could be fitted according to the circumstances of their telling. No matter how much he would deviate from the main line, he always got back on track. His stories were powerfully mnemonic, seemingly ad hoc performances.

I was asked if I would read "Dresden" in Dresden. It was a moving experience for me not least because it elicited other narratives from my audience, stories and circumstances I could never have imagined when I wrote the poem.

"Second Language" from *First Language*: My parents learned Irish as a second language, and insisted on it being the first language of the home. To that extent Irish is my first language. I suppose I learned English from the street and from the conversation of relatives. Reading the poem again, I realise how much of it refers to a vanished world. The Belfast I grew up in has changed in so many ways that I no longer know where I am in it. It's almost like a foreign city.

The form of the poem, long-lined rhyming couplets, came from my translation of Rimbaud's "Le bateau ivre", also in *First Language*. Rimbaud's poem is in alexandrine quatrains rhyming *abab*. I wanted to preserve something of that form but when I sat down to attempt it I remember spending a whole day getting nowhere until it occurred to me that I could conflate two lines into one, using the long line I had used in previous books, except with rhyme. It seemed to me that the original had a ballad-like, "As I roved out" quality which could be accommodated by such an arrangement. So perhaps one could say that "Second Language" comes from some kind of French as well as what I know of Irish, Latin and English. I think I wanted to write English as if it were a foreign language, or as a translation. Maybe it is.

"Gallipoli" from *Breaking News*: This is the first part of a seven-part poem, "The War Correspondent", and should be read in that context. This Gallipoli refers to its role in the Crimean War of 1854–1856. Many of the streets in the Falls Road area where I grew up were named after that war – Inkerman, Sevastopol, Odessa Street – as hundreds of terraced houses were built at the time to accommodate mill-workers who had flooded in from Belfast's rural hinterland. I suppose their initial experience would have been one of some confusion and alienation.

Some years ago I came across William Howard Russell's account of that war and was immediately taken by the vividness of his prose. Russell was from middle-class County Dublin stock, was educated at Trinity College and worked as a correspondent for *The Times* of London. He was described by one of the soldiers on the front as "a vulgar low Irishman, who sings a good song, drinks anyone's brandy and water and smokes as many cigars as a Jolly Good Fellow. He is just the sort of chap to get information, particularly out of youngsters."

In "The War Correspondent" I used many of Russell's original reports, sometimes paraphrased or skewed slightly to accommodate the form, sometimes interspersed with my own re-imaginings of the scene. Throughout the writing I was struck by how the havoc and confusion of that war resembles contemporary wars.

"The Shadow" from *For All We Know*: *For All We Know* is a book of two parts with thirty-five poems in each part. The titles of the poems in Part One are exactly the same as the titles of those in Part Two, in the same order, and "The Shadow" here refers to that in Part Two. Again, the poem should be read as part of a sequence, though I trust it stands alone to some extent. I had been halfway through the writing of the book when, in a conversation with Paula Meehan about its themes and tropes – which include mysterious transactions or encounters in the former East Berlin as well as Dresden, Paris and Belfast – she mentioned Herman Hesse's *The Glass Bead Game*, which I hadn't read since the 1960s. I got hold of a copy the next day and saw that it might indeed fit the context of what I was writing.

Like all the other poems in the book, the lines consist of fourteen syllables. The poems are fourteen lines long, or multiples thereof, fifty-six in this case. This constraint was a great help. What first came to mind was almost invariably improved by the search for a form of words that would fit the dimensions of the poem. I had only a hazy idea of the overall plot: that came as the poems came, and I came to think of the project as a journey into a mysterious forest of language and translation.

It strikes me that we never quite know what we are writing until we come to write it, until we are confronted with a shape that demands that we re-think what we thought we had in mind. For all we know, we know very little.

The Bomb Disposal

Is it just like picking a lock
With the slow deliberation of a funeral,
Hesitating through a darkened nave
Until you find the answer?

Listening to the malevolent tick
Of its heart, can you read
The message of the threaded veins
Like print, its body's chart?

The city is a map of the city,
Its forbidden areas changing daily.
I find myself in a crowded taxi
Making deviations from the known route,

Ending in a cul-de-sac
Where everyone breaks out suddenly
In whispers, noting the boarded windows,
The drawn blinds.

Dresden

Horse Boyle was called Horse Boyle because of his brother
    Mule;
Though why Mule was called Mule is anybody's guess. I stayed
    there once,
Or rather, I nearly stayed there once. But that's another story.
At any rate they lived in this decrepit caravan, not two miles
    out of Carrick,
Encroached upon by baroque pyramids of empty baked bean
    tins, rusts
And ochres, hints of autumn merging into twilight. Horse
    believed
They were as good as a watchdog, and to tell you the truth
You wouldn't go near the place without something falling
    over:
A minor avalanche would ensue – more like a shop bell, really.

The old-fashioned ones on string, connected to the latch,
    I think,
As you entered in, the bell would tinkle in the empty shop,
    a musk
Of scrap and turf and sweets would hit you from the gloom.
    Tobacco.
Baling wire. Twine. And, of course, shelves and pyramids of tins.
An old woman would appear from the back – there was a
    sizzling pan in there,

Somewhere, a whiff of eggs and bacon – and ask you what you
    wanted;
Or rather, she wouldn't ask; she would talk about the weather. It
    had rained
That day, but it was looking better. They had just put in the spuds.
I had only come to pass the time of day, so I bought a token
    packet of Gold Leaf.

All this time the fry was frying away. Maybe she'd a daughter
    in there
Somewhere, though I hadn't heard the neighbours talk of it; if
    anybody knew,
It would be Horse. Horse kept his ears to the ground.
And he was a great man for current affairs; he owned the only
    TV in the place.
Come dusk he'd set off on his rounds, to tell the whole
    townland the latest
Situation in the Middle East, a mortar bomb attack in
    Mullaghbawn –
The damn things never worked, of course – and so he'd tell
    the story
How in his young day it was very different. Take young Flynn,
    for instance,
Who was ordered to take this bus and smuggle some sticks of
    gelignite

Across the border, into Derry, when the RUC – or was it the RIC? –
Got wind of it. The bus was stopped, the peeler stepped on.
   Young Flynn
Took it like a man, of course: he owned up right away. He
   opened the bag
And produced the bomb, his rank and serial number. For all
   the world
Like a pound of sausages. Of course, the thing was, the peeler's
   bike
Had got a puncture, and he didn't know young Flynn from
   Adam. All he wanted
Was to get home for his tea. Flynn was in for seven years and
   learned to speak
The best of Irish. He had thirteen words for a cow in heat;
A word for the third thwart in a boat, the wake of a boat on
   the ebb tide.

He knew the extinct names of insects, flowers, why this place
   was called
Whatever: *Carrick*, for example, was *a rock*. He was damn right there –
As the man said, *When you buy meat you buy bones, when you
   buy land you buy stones.*
You'd be hard put to find a square foot in the whole bloody
   parish
That wasn't thick with flints and pebbles. To this day he could
   hear the grate
And scrape as the spade struck home, for it reminded him of
   broken bones:

Digging a graveyard, maybe – or better still, trying to dig a
	reclaimed tip
Of broken delph and crockery ware – you know that sound
	that sets your teeth on edge
When the chalk squeaks on the blackboard, or you shovel
	ashes from the stove?

Master McGinty – he'd be on about McGinty then, and
	discipline, the capitals
Of South America, Moore's *Melodies,* the Battle of Clontarf, and
*Tell me this, an educated man like you: What goes on four legs
	when it's young,*
Two legs when it's grown up, and three legs when it's old? I'd pretend
I didn't know. McGinty's leather strap would come up then,
	stuffed
With threepenny bits to give it weight and sting. Of course, it
	never did him
Any harm: *You could take a horse to water but you couldn't make
	him drink.*
He himself was nearly going on to be a priest.
And many's the young cub left the school, as wise as when he came.

Carrowkeel was where McGinty came from – *Narrow Quarter,*
	Flynn explained –
Back before the Troubles, a place that was so mean and crabbed,
Horse would have it, men were known to eat their dinner
	from a drawer.

Which they'd slide shut the minute you'd walk in.
He'd demonstrate this at the kitchen table, hunched and furtive,
     squinting
Out the window – past the teetering minarets of rust, down the
     hedge-dark aisle –
To where a stranger might appear, a passer-by, or what was maybe
     worse,
Someone he knew. Someone who wanted something. Someone
     who was hungry.
Of course who should come tottering up the lane that instant
     but his brother

Mule. I forgot to mention they were twins. They were as like two –
No, not peas in a pod, for this is not the time nor the place
     to go into
Comparisons, and this is really Horse's story, Horse who – now
     I'm getting
Round to it – flew over Dresden in the war. He'd emigrated first, to
Manchester. Something to do with scrap – redundant mill machinery,
Giant flywheels, broken looms that would, eventually, be ships,
     or aeroplanes.
He said he wore his fingers to the bone.
And so, on impulse, he had joined the RAF. He became a rear gunner.
Of all the missions, Dresden broke his heart. It reminded him
     of china.
As he remembered it, long afterwards, he could hear, or almost hear
Between the rapid desultory thunderclaps, a thousand tinkling
     echoes –

All across the map of Dresden, store-rooms full of china shivered,
    teetered
And collapsed, an avalanche of porcelain, slushing and cascading:
    cherubs,
Shepherdesses, figurines of Hope and Peace and Victory, delicate
    bone fragments.
He recalled in particular a figure from his childhood, a milkmaid
Standing on the mantelpiece. Each night as they knelt down
    for the rosary,
His eyes would wander up to where she seemed to beckon to him,
    smiling,
Offering him, eternally, her pitcher of milk, her mouth of rose
    and cream.

One day, reaching up to hold her yet again, his fingers
    stumbled, and she fell.
He lifted down a biscuit tin, and opened it.
It breathed an antique incense: things like pencils, snuff, tobacco.
His war medals. A broken rosary. And there, the milkmaid's
    creamy hand, the outstretched
Pitcher of milk, all that survived. Outside, there was a scraping
And a tittering; I knew Mule's step by now, his careful drunken
    weaving
Through the tin-stacks. I might have stayed the night, but there's
    no time
To go back to that now; I could hardly, at any rate, pick up the thread.
I wandered out through the steeples of rust, the gate that was a
    broken bed.

Second Language

English not being yet a language, I wrapped my lubber-lips
    around my thumb;
Brain-deaf as an embryo, I was snuggled in my comfort-
    blanket dumb.

Growling figures campaniled above me, and twanged their
    carillons of bronze
Sienna consonants embedded with the vowels *alexandrite*,
    emerald and *topaz*.

The topos of their discourse seemed to do with me and
    convoluted genealogy;
Wordy whorls and braids and skeins and spiral helices,
    unskeletoned from laminate geology –

How this one's slate-blue gaze is correspondent to
    another's new-born eyes;
Gentians, forget-me-nots, and cornflowers, diurnal in a
    heliotrope surmise.

Alexandrine tropes came gowling out like beagles, loped and
    unroped
On a snuffly Autumn. Nimrod followed after with his bold
    Arapahoes,

Who whooped and hollered in their unforked tongue. The
    trail was starred with
Myrrh and frankincense of Anno Domini; the Wise Men wisely
    paid their tariff.

A single star blazed at my window. Crepuscular, its acoustic
    perfume dims
And swells like flowers on the stanzaic-papered wall. Shipyard
    hymns

Then echoed from the East: gantry-clank and rivet-ranks, Six-
    County hexametric
Brackets, bulkheads, girders, beams, and stanchions; convocated
    and Titanic.

Leviathans of rope snarled out from ropeworks: disgorged
    hawsers, unkinkable lay,
Ratlines, S-twists, plaited halyards, Z-twists, catlines; all had their
    say.

Tobacco-scent and snuff breathed out in gouts of factory
    smoke like aromatic camomile;
Sheaves of brick-built mill-stacks glowered in the sulphur-
    mustard fog like campaniles.

The dim bronze noise of midnight-noon and Angelus then
  boomed and clinked in Latin
Conjugations; statues wore their shrouds of amaranth; the
  thurible chinked out its smoky patina.

I inhaled *amo, amas, amat* in quids of *pros* and *versus* and
  Introibos
Ad altare Dei; incomprehensibly to others, spoke in Irish. I
  slept through the Introit.

The enormous Monastery surrounded me with nave
  and architrave. Its ornate pulpit
Spoke to me in fleurs-de-lys of Purgatory. Its sacerdotal gaze
  became my pupil.

My pupil's nose was bathed in Pharaonic unguents of dope
  and glue.
Flimsy tissue-paper plans of aeroplanes unfolded whimsical
  ideas of the blue,

Where, unwound, the prop's elastic is unpropped and balsa-
  wood extends its wings
Into the hazardous azure of April. It whirrs into the realm of
  things.

Things are kinks that came in tubes; like glue or paint
  extruded, that became
A hieroglyphic alphabet. Incestuous in pyramids, Egyptians
  were becalmed.

I climbed into it, delved its passageways, its sepulchral
    interior, its things of kings
Embalmed; sarcophagi, whose perfume I exhumed in chancy
    versions of the *I-Ching*.

A chink of dawn was revelated by the window. Far-off cocks
    crowed crowingly
And I woke up, verbed and tensed with speaking English; I
    lisped the words so knowingly.

I love the as-yet morning, when no one's abroad, and I am like
    a postman on his walk,
Distributing strange messages and bills, and arbitrations with
    the world of talk:

I foot the snow and almost-dark. My shoes are crisp, and bite
    into the blue-
White firmament of pavement. My father holds my hand and
    goes blah-

Blah with me into the ceremonial dawn. I'm wearing tweed.
    The universe is Lent
And Easter is an unspun cerement, the gritty, knitty, tickly
    cloth of unspent

Time. I feel its warp and weft. Bobbins pirn and shuttle in
    Imperial
Typewriterspeak. I hit the keys. The ribbon-black clunks out the
    words in serial.

What comes next is next, and no one knows the *che sera* of
    it, but must allow
The *Tipp-Ex* present at the fingertips. Listen now: an angel
    whispers of the here-and-now.

The future looms into the mouth incessantly, gulped-at
    and unspoken;
Its guardian is intangible, but gives you hints and winks
    and nudges as its broken token.

I woke up blabbering and dumb with too much sleep. I
    rubbed my eyes and ears.
I closed my eyes again and flittingly, forgetfully, I glimpsed
    the noise of years.

Gallipoli
(from "The War Correspondent")

Take sheds and stalls from Billingsgate,
glittering with scaling-knives and fish,
the tumbledown outhouses of English farmers' yards
that reek of dung and straw, and horses
cantering the mewsy lanes of Dublin;

take an Irish landlord's ruinous estate,
elaborate pagodas from a Chinese Delftware dish
where fishes fly through shrouds and sails and yards
of leaking ballast-laden junks bound for Benares
in search of bucket-loads of tea as black as tin;

take a dirty gutter from a back street in Boulogne,
where shops and houses teeter so their pitched roofs
    meet,
some chimney stacks as tall as those in Sheffield
or Irish round towers,
smoking like a fleet of British ironclad destroyers;

take the garlic-oregano-tainted arcades of Bologna,
linguini-twists of souks and smells of rotten meat,
as labyrinthine as the rifle-factories of Springfield,
or the tenements deployed by bad employers
who sit in parlours doing business drinking *Power's*;

then populate this slum with Cypriot and Turk,
Armenians and Arabs, British riflemen
and French Zouaves, camel-drivers, officers, and sailors,
sappers, miners, Nubian slaves, Greek money-changers,
plus interpreters who do not know the lingo;

dress them in turbans, shawls of fancy needlework,
fedoras, fezzes, sashes, shirts of fine Valenciennes,
boleros, pantaloons designed by jobbing tailors,
knickerbockers of the ostrich and the pink flamingo,
sans-culottes, and outfits even stranger;

requisition slaughter-houses for the troops,
and stalls with sherbet, lemonade, and rancid lard
        for sale,
a temporary hospital or two, a jail,
a stagnant harbour redolent with cholera,
and open sewers running down the streets;

let the staple diet be green cantaloupes
swarming with flies washed down with sour wine,
accompanied by the Byzantine
jangly music of the cithara
and the multi-lingual squawks of parakeets –

O landscape riddled with the diamond mines of Kimberley,
and all the oubliettes of Trebizond,
where opium-smokers doze among the Persian rugs,
and spies and whores in dim-lit snugs
discuss the failing prowess of the Allied powers,

where prowling dogs sniff for offal beyond
the stench of pulped plums and apricots,
from which is distilled the brandy they call "grape-shot",
and soldiers lie dead or drunk among the crushed flowers –
I have not even begun to describe Gallipoli.

The Shadow

The Glass Bead Game? I said. *Das Glasperlenspiel,* if you like,
you said, not that my German is anything to speak of.

Though I remember, as a verb, *perlen* means to bubble,
as in upwardly streaming pearls of water in a pot

just coming to the boil. As for what went on in the book,
I'm at a loss to say what it was all about, or not.

The game itself was difficult to visualize. I thought
of a chess more infinitely complicated than chess,

played in three dimensions, if not four or five, for the game,
as I understood it, could admit of most anything,

though politics was frowned on. The game was above all
that.
A Bach motet, or how the prose style of Julius Caesar

mirrors the cadences of some Early Byzantine hymns,
the calligraphic gestures of a flock of birds at dusk:

these were considered subjects for the Glass Bead Game. Or not.
There were always those who thought the opposite to be true.

The subject of the book becomes a *Magister Ludi,*
Master of the Game. He is skilled in many disciplines.

With a luminous gold stylus he writes a hieroglyph
on the dark, and so initiates a constellation

from which blossom countless others. Were the Game a
    music,
it would require an organ with an infinite number

of manuals, pedals and stops. If geometry, or not,
Pythagoras never dreamed of it. Plato was not close.

Though it originated in the simple abacus,
the wires representing a musical staff and the beads

of various sizes, shapes and colours of glass the notes,
it grew in time to be a model of the universe.

I gather the glass beads became metaphorical beads,
not to be fingered by hand but tuned to some other

At any rate, a Master is not allowed to marry.
Now I remember this one was called Knecht, which means
    not knight

but vassal. He is in thrall to the Game. He is assigned
an underling, a Shadow. The Shadow must study him.

It does not do for a Master to have a weak Shadow.
And the Master must be fit to stand up to his Shadow.

Though the Shadow may act in his master's stead, he may
    not
lay forward proposals of his own. And though he may wear

the Master's robes when occasion demands he can never
be Master himself. Such are the rules of the Glass Bead
    Game.

So you must cultivate your Shadow, for there is never
one Master, but another lies waiting in his shadow,

you said. And what has all of this got to do with Berlin,
I said, and your time there? You don't know how much I
    missed you.

I kept wondering where you were and what you were
    thinking.
As did I of you, you don't know the half of it, you said.

Isn't that the trouble? That I don't know the half of it?
Sometimes I wonder if we speak the same language, I said.

You took a sip of cold coffee and stared out the window.
The sun had just come out. Leaf-shadow dappled the cobbles.

It's like this, you said. Those who play the Glass Bead Game
    don't know
there's a war on they're so wrapped up in themselves and their
    Game.

You know I was in Berlin for a reason. Yes, I chose
to walk that path, as surely as I chose to go with you.

There's no point in going into what else I might have been.
Then you walked out the door and I followed in your shadow.

THEO DORGAN

All I can say for sure about the genesis of a poem is that I always experience it as incoming news from otherwhere. Robert Graves once said that a poem grows from a small verbal nucleus that somehow takes root in your attention, gradually accumulating force and form as it moves to the forefront of consciousness in a state of mind that he calls "an analeptic trance". That tallies with my own experience, and these five poems draw what power they may have from that moment of emergence; each is, you might say, its own authority. Unless a poem intrudes itself, speaks itself, into my attention I don't bother writing it. None of this, of course, precludes variousness – which is why I have chosen five very different kinds of poem here.

There is, perhaps, another way of saying this: I have never written a poem deliberately, in the sense that I have never sat down and said to myself, OK, I think I'll write a poem about this or that or the other thing. Unless the poem has been buried in there somewhere, muttering itself to itself, I don't write it.

There is a kind of collision principle at work here: on the one hand I am immersed in language in much the same way as I am immersed in air; on the other hand, I have a contingent life, particular to me, a life on the event plain, as it were. The five poems here come out of a spark leaping from language to life-event, or vice versa. And after that comes craft, the long engagement with form, the effort to house the poem in time.

Kilmainham Gaol, Dublin, Easter 1991

for Frank Harte

Roadies in ponytails stringing lights and cables,
a beer can popped in the corner, echo of sound check.
Outside in the filling yard, hum of expectation.

We pour through the narrow gate under the gallows hook
in twos and threes, becoming an audience.
Before the lights go down we examine each other shyly.

The singer surveys his audience, heat rising
to the tricolour and Plough overhead.
As the first words of Galvin's lament climb to invoke
James Connolly's ghost, we are joined by the dead.

I say this as calmly as I can. The gaunt dead
crowded the catwalks, shirtsleeved, disbelieving.
The guards had long since vanished, but these
looked down on us, their faces pale.

I saw men there who had never made their peace,
men who had failed these many years to accept their fate,
still stunned by gunfire, wounds, fear for their families;
paralysed until now by the long volleys of May so long ago.

I think that we all felt it, their doubt and their new fear,
the emblems so familiar, the setting, our upturned faces,
so unreal. Only the dignity of the singer's art
had power to release them. I felt it, I say this calmly.

I saw them leave, in twos and threes, as the song ended.
I do not know that there is a heaven but I saw their souls
fan upward like leaves from a dry book, sped out into the
    night
by volleys of applause; sped out, I hope, into some light at
    last.

I do not know that I will ever be the same again.
That soft-footed gathering of the dead into their peace
was like something out of a book. In Kilmainham Gaol
I saw this. I felt this. I say this as calmly and as lovingly as
    I can.

Seven Versions of Loss Eternal

1

Imagine the salt caking an evening sand-rose,
a steep dune sprawling towards the infinite,
a lone traveller trying hard not to fall –
lost in the sands, hallucinating trinities –
imagine his thirst for reconciling fountains,
for the three jets made one in the sun's blind strobe,
for the three paths rounding to where she waits.

2

Green cracked linoleum, the oak door shredding
wind and rain-dark into spindrift,
dust and hot paint behind him, the day's labour
already lost in a settling of files. Hand on his collar
he pauses a moment, irresolute, almost lost
but she is not there, never will be again. A paper clip
clicks against change in his pocket, and here's his bus.

3

What is must be like from space, imagine,
the child's nightmare downwardness, the globe
blue, green and watered, the great mountains
scored like ribs across a carcase, cities
winking on and off, deltas a great scrawl
of mud and silt on the blue-green flush of silk –
to be *there* and never to go down again.

4

The projector ticks as it cools, metal and glass
going lifeless with electricity shut off. His hand
spins with the deadweight of the rewind arms,
his mind as vacant as the cinema far below.
In the tang of hot celluloid he hesitates to think
of where he might go now there is nowhere to go,
a man becoming a shadow of himself.

5

Imagine the great Atlantic waves, rearing to freeze
far over him – embattled and stubborn, raw from spray
and cold and drenching, the radio gone, the stars unseen
for days now, unable for even a moment to go below;
a rag of topsail's enough to drive him on, harder and deeper
by the minute, as long as his wrists hold out.
Her blue handkerchief wound around his watchstrap.

6

Salt on the butcher block of beech, he leans hard
on his circling hands, the brush scouring the work away
in the blue light from the window. He has learned
not to breathe too deeply in this quiet time, never
to look at his hands until he has scrubbed them clean.
He clicks off the light with his back to the street,
the most terrifying moment of his day.

7

Imagine your whole day is a search for a missing sign –
you scan rivers of paper, faces drifted in the streets,
magazine illustrations, cinema posters, the blank
windows of schools, offices, factories. You listen
to bus tyres in the rain, at night you sneak sudden glances
at clouds ripping past the stars. Nothing.
An irregular contraction in the chest. Nothing.

On a Day Far from Now

Death will come and have your eyes
And I will go into her arms
Without fear or hesitation.

Frost on the slates
Of our beloved square,
The cars riding low under
A hurrying sky when

I open the great hall door
And take her hand,
Her long black coat.

The bare-flagged hallway, frost
And perfume on the night air.

I watch her let down
Her gleaming hair,
Open her slender arms
In your exact gesture.

Death will come and have your eyes
And I will go into her arms
Without fear or hesitation.

Ithaca

for Leonard Cohen

When you set out from Ithaca again,
let it be autumn, early, the plane leaves falling as
    you go,
for spring would shake you with its quickening,
its whispers of youth.

You will have earned the road down to the harbour,
duty discharged, your toll of labour paid,
the house four-square, your son in the full of
    fatherhood,
his mother, your long-beloved, gone to the shades.

Walk by the doorways, do not look left or right,
do not inhale the woodsmoke,
the shy glow of the young girls,
the resin and pine of home.
Allow them permit you to leave,
they have been good neighbours.

Plank fitted to plank, slow work and sure,
the mast straight as your back.
Water and wine, oil, salt and bread.
Take a hand in yours for luck.

Cast off the lines without a backward glance
and sheet in the sail.
There will be harbours, shelter from weather,
There will be long empty passages far from land.
There may be love or kindness, do not count on this
but allow for the possibility.
Be ready for storms.

When you take leave of Ithaca, round to the south
then strike far down for Circe, Calypso,
what you remember, what you must keep in mind.
Trust to your course, long since laid down for you.
There was never any question of turning back.
All those who came the journey with you,
those who fell to the flash of bronze,
those who turned away into other fates,
are long gathered to asphodel and dust.
You will go uncompanioned, but go you must

There will be time in the long days and nights,
stunned by the sun or driven by the stars,
to unwind your spool of life.
You will learn again what you always knew –
the wind sweeps everything away.

When you set out from Ithaca again,
you will not need to ask where you are going.
Give every day your full, unselfconscious attention –
the rise and flash of the swell on your beam,
the lift into small harbours –
and do not forget Ithaca, keep Ithaca in your mind.
All that it was and is, and will be without you.

Be grateful for where you have been,
for those who kept to your side,
those who strode out ahead of you
or stood back and watched you sail away.
Be grateful for kindness in the perfumed dark
but sooner or later you will sail out again.

Some morning, some clear night,
you will come to the Pillars of Hercules.
Sail through if you wish. You are free to turn back.
Go forward on deck, lay your hand on the mast,
hear the wind in its dipping branch.
Now you are free of home and journeying,
rocked on the cusp of tides.
Ithaca is before you, Ithaca is behind you.
Man is born homeless, and shaped for the sea.
You must do what is best.

Thornship

A thornship lifted from the blown hedge,
white rags to carry her head
and a wren her pilot.

High in the blue of March a hawk wheeled
out of the archaic, and a crow's rattle
dragged back along her wake.

I set my heart to follow her lift,
shifting my ground as to the manner born –
borne up and out with her,

the spume of blossom dusting my eyes.
The wind thrummed in her rigging,
the wren dropped back

along her broad track and she dipped for the north,
a fine strain in her ribs, her decking
meticulously fit.

How long she rose and where she carried us,
what we saw from that height, how many
we were, and from where,

doesn't matter now. Dream up alongside,
my salty love of May, settle your feathers
here beside me, fit for the journey.

PAUL DURCAN

I chose these five poems because I stand by them. They achieve the technique of poetry which, as Pushkin so often wrote, is to keep in touch with prose.

The Death by Heroin of Sid Vicious

There – but for the clutch of luck – go I.

At daybreak – in the arctic fog of a February daybreak –
Shoulderlength helmets in the watchtowers of the
    concentration camp
Caught me out in the intersecting arcs of the swirling
    searchlights:

There were at least a zillion of us caught out there
– Like ladybirds under a boulder –
But under the microscope each of us was unique,

Unique and we broke for cover, crazily breasting
The barbed wire and some of us made it
To the forest edge, but many of us did not

Make it, although their unborn children did –
Such as you whom the camp commandant branded
Sid Vicious of the Sex Pistols. Jesus, break his fall:

There – but for the clutch of luck – go we all.

"Windfall", 8 Parnell Hill, Cork

But, then, at the end of the day I could always say
– Well, now, I am going home:
I felt elected, steeped, sovereign to be able to say –
I am going home.
When I was at home I liked to stay at home;
At home I stayed at home for weeks;
At home I used sit in a winged chair by the window
Overlooking the river and the factory chimneys,
The electricity power station and the car assembly works,
The fleets of trawlers and the pilot tugs,
Dreaming that life is a dream which is real,
The river a reflection of itself in its own waters,
Goya sketching Goya among the smoky mirrors.
The industrial vista was my Mont Sainte-Victoire;
While my children sat on my knees watching TV
Their mother, my wife, reclined on the couch
Knitting a bright-coloured scarf, drinking a cup of black coffee,
Smoking a cigarette – one of her own roll-ups.
I closed my eyes and breathed in and breathed out.
It is ecstasy to breathe if you are at home in the world.
What a windfall! A home of our own!
Our neighbours' houses had names like "Con Amore",
"Sans Souci", "Pacelli", "Montini", "Homesville";
But we called our home "Windfall":
"Windfall", 8 Parnell Hill, Cork.
In the gut of my head coursed the leaf of tranquility

Which I dreamed was known only to Buddhist Monks
In lotus monasteries high up in the Hindu Kush.
Down here in the dark depths of Ireland,
Below sea-level in the city of Cork,
In a city as intimate and homicidal as a Little Marseilles,
In a country where all the children of the nation
Are not cherished equally
And where the best go homeless, while the worst
Erect block-house palaces – self-regardingly ugly
Having a home of your own can give to a family
A chance in a lifetime to transcend death.

At the high window, shipping from all over the world
Being borne up and down the busy, yet contemplative,
      river;
Skylines drifting in and out of skylines in the cloudy valley;
Firelight at dusk, and city lights in the high window,
Beyond them the control tower of the airport on the hill
– A lighthouse in the sky flashing green to white to green;
Our black-and-white cat snoozing in the corner of a chair;
Pastels and etchings on the four walls, and over the
      mantelpiece
Van Gogh's Grave and *Lovers in Water*,
A room wallpapered in books and family photograph albums
Chronicling the adventures and metamorphoses of family life:
In swaddling clothes in Mammy's arms on baptism day;
Being a baby of nine months and not remembering it;
Face-down in a pram, incarcerated in a high chair;

Everybody, including strangers, wearing shop-window smiles;
With Granny in Felixstowe, with Granny in Ballymaloe;
In a group photo in First Infants, on a bike at thirteen;
In the back garden in London, in the back garden in
    Cork;
Performing a headstand after First Holy Communion;
Getting a kiss from the Bishop on Confirmation Day;
Straw hats in the Bois de Boulogne, wearing wings at
    the seaside;
Mammy and Daddy holding hands on the Normandy
    Beaches;
Mammy and Daddy at the wedding of Jeremiah and Margot;
Mammy and Daddy queuing up for *Last Tango in Paris*;
Boating on the Shannon, climbing mountains in Kerry;
Building sandcastles in Killala, camping in Barley Cove;
Picnicking in Moone, hide-and-go-seek in Clonmacnoise;
Riding horses, cantering, jumping fences;
Pushing out toy yachts in the pond in the Tuileries;
The Irish College revisited in the Rue des Irlandais;
Sipping an *orange pressé* through a straw on the roof of the
    Beaubourg;
Dancing in Pere Lachaise, weeping at Auvers.
Year in, year out, I pored over these albums accumulating,
My children looking over my shoulder, exhilarated as I was,
Their mother presiding at our ritual from a distance
– The far side of the hearthrug, diffidently, proudly:
Schoolbooks on the floor and pyjamas on the couch –
Whose turn is it tonight to put the children to bed?

Our children swam about our home
As if it was their private sea,
Their own unique, symbiotic fluid
Of which their parents also partook.
Such is home – a sea of your own –
In which you hang upside down from the ceiling
With equanimity, while postcards from Thailand on the
        mantelpiece
Are raising their eyebrow markings benignly:
Your hands dangling their prayers to the floorboards of your
        home,
Sifting the sands underneath the surfaces of conversations,
The marine insect life of the family psyche.
A home of your own – or a sea of your own –
In which climbing the walls is as natural
As making love on the stairs;
In which when the telephone rings
Husband and wife are metamorphosed into smiling accomplices,
Both declining to answer it;
Initiating, instead, a yet more subversive kiss
– A kiss they have perhaps never attempted before –
And might never have dreamed of attempting
Were it not for the telephone belling.
Through the banisters or along the banister rails
The pyjama-clad children solemnly watching
Their parents at play, jump up and down in support,
Race back to bed, gesticulating wordlessly:
The most subversive unit in society is the human family.

We're almost home, pet, almost home . . .
Our home is at . . .
I'll be home . . .
I have to go home now . . .
I want to go home now . . .
Are you feeling homesick? . . .
Are you anxious to get home? . . .
I can't wait to get home . . .
Let's stay at home tonight and . . .
What time will you be coming home at? . . .
If I'm not home by six at the latest, I'll phone . . .
We're nearly home, don't worry, we're nearly home . . .

But then with good reason
I was put out of my home:
By a keen wind felled.
I find myself now without a home
Having to live homeless in the alien, foreign city of Dublin.
It is an eerie enough feeling to be homesick
Yet knowing you will be going home next week;
It is an eerie feeling beyond all ornithological analysis
To be homesick knowing that there is no home to go
    home to:
Day by day, creeping, crawling,
Moonlighting, escaping,
Bed-and-breakfast to bed-and-breakfast;
Hostels, centres, one-night hotels.

Homeless in Dublin,
Blown about the suburban streets at evening,
Peering in the windows of other people's homes
Wondering what it must feel like
To be sitting around a fire –
Apache or Cherokee or Bourgeoisie –
Beholding the firelit faces of your family,
Beholding their starry or their TV gaze:
Windfall to Windfall – can you hear me?
Windfall to Windfall . . .
We're almost home pet, don't worry anymore, we're almost
    home.

Diarrhoea Attack at Party Headquarters in Leningrad

An attack of diarrhoea at Party Headquarters in
    Leningrad
Was not something I imagined ever happening to me
Which is perhaps partly why it did happen to me.
The presidium had barely taken its place
Under the iconic portraits of V. I. Lenin and M. S. Gorbachev
When I could feel the initial missiles
Firing down the sky of my stomach
Setting in motion something that was irreversible –
The *realpolitik* of the irreversible.
The only consolation was that I was wearing
    underpants.
The fact is that sometimes I do not wear underpants.
Oddly enough I was wearing red underpants
Which I had originally purchased in Marks &
    Spencer's.
The first explosion resulted in immediate
    devastation –
The ensuing explosions serving only to define
The innately irreversible dialectic of catastrophe.
I whispered magnanimously into the earhole of my
    interpreter.
He reciprocated that since he also had "a trauma of the
    intestine"

We should both take our leave *immédiatement* and he
    showed me
Such fraternal solicitude that in my mind's eye
I can still see Lenin peering down at me
As if he were peering down at nobody else in the hall.
A black Volga whisked us back to our hotel and ignominy –
– My ignominy – not anybody else's ignominy – and that
    night
Over cups of tea we discussed the war in Afghanistan,
Agreeing that realistically it appeared an insoluble problem,
Yet hoping against hope that somehow it would be solved
And that – as you put it, Slava – "Russian boys come home."
There is nothing necessarily ignominious about anything.

Our Father

I was going over to Mummy's place for lunch.
I had said my morning prayers
But I had not expected
My morning prayers materially to alter the day.
Our Father who art in heaven
(Daddy had died two winters ago)
Hallowed be Thy name, Thy kingdom come,
Thy will be done on earth as it is in heaven.

I had decided to catch the number 13 bus to
    Palmerston Park
From outside Dáil Éireann in Kildare Street
But at the last moment I changed my mind
And I caught the number 14 bus to Dartry.
I do not know why I changed my mind.
Possibly it was because the number 14 came first
Or possibly it was because of the memory
That Daddy, when he was alive, appeared to be
    perplexed
That I never came home by the number 14 route.
He seemed to think that I should come home by
    the number 14 route
And that it was a crime against nature
To come home by the number 13 route.

I sat at the back of the bus on the lower deck
With two bunches of flowers for Mummy in my lap.
When I became aware that the conductor was staring at me
We were stopped outside the National Concert Hall and I
    thought:
Maybe he likes the look of me.
He commented: "I like your irises."
"What?"
"Your irises – I like your irises."
The conductor swayed above me, a knowing smile in his
    eyes,
As the double decker lurched around Kelly's Corner –
A landmark of Daddy's
Because on it stood a pub called The Bleeding Horse.
It was the name that attracted him.
He was never inside it in his life.
Every time we drove past The Bleeding Horse
I stared at the blood trickling out of the white mare's
    withers,
All menstruation and still life.
"I love flowers" – the conductor continued,
Licking the baton of his forefinger
"My wife says I'm mad and of course I am.
I am mad about flowers.
Lovely irises you have – let me touch them.
I have my own greenhouse – the width of this bus.
My father-in-law built it for me donkey's years ago.
My orchids are in bloom at the moment.

If I'd my way, I'd have nothing but orchids.
All the same a man's got to be pragmatic."
He clung lithely to the vertical rail as the driver
Flew the bus over Portobello Bridge.

"I've aubergines, peppers, tomatoes, lettuce.
The neighbours are keen on my iceberg lettuce.
They're always pestering me also for my courgettes.
Cucumber too – but you have to be cautious with
    cucumber.
What with the way the males pollinate the females
You've got to be terribly cautious with your stamens.
Cucumbers are very much that way inclined:
Proliferation, proclivities, you never know where you are.
I have to keep all my cacti on the upper shelves."

As we slowed down near Rathmines Town Hall, senior
    citizens
On Free Travel called out to the conductor to collect fares.
"Do your duty now, Mister, and collect fares."
But he waved to the passengers who were disembarking,
A wave that was at once a valediction and a benediction:
"I am not collecting fares this morning," he confided in me,
"There are times in public transport when it is more
    auspicious
Not to collect fares and today is an auspicious day.
I adore my greenhouse. It can get so hot inside it.
Anything more than a pair of shorts and I'm scalded

'Where'd you get your tan?' – the neighbour woman asks me.
'In my greenhouse, where else?' – I answer her back.
A perfect lie.
She wags her finger at my magnolia in the front garden
And she teases me: 'Oh, a cherry blossom
Is good enough for the rest of us but not for the likes of
    you.
For the likes of you it has to be a *magnolium* no less.
Only a *magnolium* is good enough for the likes of you.'
That's what she calls it – a *magnolium*."

We were whizzing past the pharmacy on Upper Rathmines
    Road
And the Church of Ireland Teacher Training College
But he wanted to dwell on his magnolia:
"It's not a real word at all, you know, 'magnolia'.
There was a Frenchman – Magnol was his name –
From a place called Montpellier. My wife knew a man
From Montpellier – that's how I remember it.
But I do like your irises.

You have to be patient in this game
And it can be so tedious on top of that.
My grapes, for example. Grapes are too excitable.
I have to keep each grape separate from the other.
Time-consuming it is
Keeping all my grapes separate from each other.
Each grape has to be totally separate from the next grape

And only a few weeks ago I lost fifty pounds' worth
Of azaleas – wiped out by Jack Frost.
When I'm skedaddling off to the depot I ask the
    wife
To remember to open the greenhouse window
But if she remembers to open it,
Sure as not she will forget to close it.
You know what wives are like – not to mention
    husbands.
At the moment, actually, I'm all sweet pea."
I apologised to him as I dismounted at Dartry.
"Sorry, but I have to get out at this stop."
"Don't be sorry – be nice to your irises."

As the bus swerved away from the kerb, I thought:
Amn't I the lucky breadman that I got the Dartry
    bus
Instead of the Palmerston Park bus,
The number 14 instead of the number 13?
The conductor waved to me as the bus picked up
    speed.
I looked about me on the street to check if anybody
    was looking.
I blessed myself.
Our Father who art in heaven
I could feel the conductor's knees brush against my lips
As he ran his fingers through the clay of my hair.

Under the chestnuts and the pine trees and the copper
  beeches
I walk down the street where Daddy slipped on the ice.
He had lain here until a gas worker had found him
And put him in an ambulance and waved goodbye to him,
A gas worker with a piece of piping in his hand.

I press the bell to Mummy's apartment.
I stare up into the surveillance camera lens.
I am a suspect in an interrogation centre,
A forty-five-year-old amoeba dwindling under a
  microscope.
When a light bulb flashes and her voice crackles over
The intercom I know she can perceive
The panic in the pupils of her son's eyes.
After lunch – soup, a chop, potatoes and peas –
She says that she does not understand my new book
  of poems
Which are poems I have composed for my dead father.
"But" – she smiles knowingly – "I like your irises."

Rosie Joyce

I

That was that Sunday afternoon in May
When a hot sun pushed through the clouds
And you were born!

I was driving the two hundred miles from west to
    east,
The sky blue-and-white china in the fields
In impromptu picnics of tartan rugs;

When neither words nor I
Could have known that you had been named
    already
And that your name was Rosie –

Rosie Joyce! May you some day in May
Fifty-six years from today be as lucky
As I was when you were born that Sunday:

To drive such side-roads, such main roads, such
    ramps, such roundabouts,
To cross such bridges, to by-pass such villages, such
    towns
As I did on your Incarnation Day.

By-passing Swinford – Croagh Patrick in my rear-view
    mirror –
My mobile rang and, stopping on the hard edge of
    P. Flynn's highway,
I heard Mark your father say:

"A baby girl was born at 3.33 p.m.
Weighing 7 and 1/2 lbs in Holles Street.
Tough work, all well."

II

That Sunday in May before daybreak
Night had pushed up through the slopes of Achill
Yellow forefingers of Arum Lily – the first of the
    year;

Down at the Sound the first rhododendrons
Purpling the golden camps of whins;
The first hawthorns powdering white the mainland;

The first yellow irises flagging roadside streams;
Quills of bog-cotton skimming the bogs;
Burrishoole cemetery shin-deep in forget-me-nots;

The first sea pinks speckling the seashore;
Cliffs of London Pride, groves of bluebell,
First fuchsia, Queen Anne's Lace, primrose.

I drove the Old Turlough Road, past Walter Durcan's
 Farm,
Umbrella'd in the joined handwriting of its ash trees;
I drove Tulsk, Kilmainham, the Grand Canal.

Never before had I felt so fortunate
To be driving back into Dublin city;
Each canal bridge an old pewter brooch.

I rode the waters and the roads of Ireland,
Rosie, to be with you, seashell at my ear!
How I laughed when I cradled you in my hand.

Only at Tarmonbarry did I slow down,
As in my father's Ford Anglia half a century ago
He slowed down also, as across the River Shannon

We crashed, rattled and bounced on a Bailey bridge;
Daddy relishing his role as Moses,
Enunciating the name of the Great Divide

Between the East and the West!
We are the people of the West,
Our fate to go East.

No such thing, Rosie, as a Uniform Ireland
And please God there never will be;
There is only the River Shannon and all her sister rivers

And all her brother mountains and their family prospects.
There are higher powers than politics
And these we call wildflowers or, geologically, people.

Rosie Joyce – that Sunday in May
Not alone did you make my day, my week, my year
To the prescription of Jonathan Philbin Bowman –

Daymaker!
Daymaker!
Daymaker!

Popping out of my daughter, your mother –
Changing the expressions on the faces all around you –
All of them looking like blue hills in a heat haze –

But you saved my life. For three years
I had been subsisting in the slums of despair,
Unable to distinguish one day from the next.

III

On the return journey from Dublin to Mayo
In Charlestown on Main Street
I meet John Normanly, organic farmer from Curry.

He is driving home to his wife Caroline
From a Mountbellew meeting of the Western Development
    Commission
Of Dillon House in Ballaghadereen.

He crouches in his car, I waver in the street,
As we exchange lullabies of expectancy;
We wet our foreheads in John Moriarty's autobiography.

The following Sunday is the Feast of the Ascension
Of Our Lord into Heaven:
Thank You, O Lord, for the Descent of Rosie onto Earth.

PETER FALLON

MINUTES

I appreciate the invitation to be part of this enterprise – selecting a handful of poems and writing about my choices. As is so often the case, there's a long way to do this, and a short one. And frequently the outcome of whichever way is chosen is not much different.

I remember years ago when an American friend of mine, a most thoughtful, deliberate man, was asked to prepare a volume of his *Selected Poems*. He pondered and weighed with typical care the ways he might approach the undertaking – what poems to include, whether to excerpt from longer poems and sequences, whether or not to make revisions, and how to arrange the arc of the book. I'm sure he made a list. He probably slept on various ideas. He probably made another list and then, because he was struggling, he sought advice from another friend, A.A. Ammons.

"You, Archie, you've been through this process. Do you mind if I ask how long it took you?"

And Ammons replied: "Oh, Wendell, I'd say about forty minutes."

I work slowly. I don't seem to have many poems. For years and years my work attended to a particular place, a few square miles between my home place near Kells and my home in Loughcrew in North Meath. Perhaps inevitably the poems employed and responded to the history and language, the idiom and, even, the vocabulary of certain experiences there. And sometimes it felt as if there was too much to explain in them. The need to gloss them felt like a burden. I wanted to write more simply. When I finished "Gate" I thought I might have started to do just that. Though it has a serious flaw, I find myself still standing over it.

The other poems are newer. I've been surprised to discover that we don't learn how to write poems. Well, we could, I suppose. But that would be, I suspect, to find a formula for writing the same poem over and over. If we're lucky we learn not how to write poems – but to write a poem, the one we're working on. And then when it's finished we've to start, and learn, again. I like to think "Go", "The Company of Horses" and "The Less Ado" are samples of poems which resolved themselves.

And perhaps because I write so few poems I am grateful for them and the newest ones mean more to me. I like to think "After a Storm" has something (not that I'd dream of comparing myself with the American master) of a Frost narrative, one of those magical poems of his which have a veneer of pure music and an undertow of unfathomable mystery, something, say, like his enchanting "The Impulse" (from "The Hill Wife"). More important than liking my poem, or hoping it's impressive or admirable or anything like that, I find myself trusting it. And that for the moment would seem to do.

Go

Then go beyond the reach
of road, lane,
beaten path, or set
of single prints,
deep into the realm
of stillness.

There you bear
the sores and sorrows
of a neighbour,
the illness
of a friend.
There a rock-

pool convalesces
at once after
a spill of rain.
Look out
where landfall
coalesces

with the sea's
sheet iron
and see yourself
for that split
second before
the wind's blade

shreds
the mirror of the bay.
Nothing has stalled
that sound
the length of time.
On any day,

in any weather,
those shards and shatters
glisten.
The morning is telling
you
your life. Listen.

The Company of Horses

They are flesh on the bones
of the wind, going full gallop,
the loan of freedom.
But the company of broken

horses is a quiet blessing.
Just to walk in the paddock;
to stand by their stall.
Left to their own devices

they graze or doze, hock to fetlock
crooked at ease, or – head to tail –
nibble withers, hips and flanks.
They fit themselves flat

to the ground. They roll.
But the mere sound or smell
of us – and they're all neighs
and nickerings, their snorts

the splinters of the waves.
And growing out of morning
mists the ghosts of night
form silhouettes along the ridge,

a dun, two chestnuts,
and a bay. A shy colt stares
and shivers — a trembling like
fine feathers in a sudden breeze

around the hooves of heavy
horses. And the dam,
with foal to foot, steadies herself
to find her bearings,

her ears antennae of attention.
Put your hand towards her head-
collar, whispering your *Ohs* and *Whoa*,
Oh the boy and *Oh the girl*,

close your eyes and lean
your head towards
her quiet head,
the way the old grey mare,

hearing that her hero
joined the sleep
of death, spread her mane
across his breast and began to wail and weep.

After a Storm

It took days
for the waves

to recover,
to re-form

their orderly queue
to land.

Then she said,
I'm not the better

of it yet,
and who knows when

I'll over it.
All I know is

I'm ownlier
than I ever thought.

He'd been
good as gold

all the while since,
a shield

to ward off
blows of grief.

It's where we are
now, and these

are our lives,
he said,

as he looked
to the sea –

but a wave
to hand

simply shrugged,
then turned its back

on their separate selves.

The Less Ado

Even as a butterfly's
spread wings, a lake so still,
so clear the image
of the hill

beyond,
you strained to trace
the seam of which is which,
their meeting place,

so the ripple
when it happened
(and it always had to happen)
was a breath of wind

made visible.
Now time's what you've
less of and a friend's
in hospital you move

closer to the gospel
that night
might be best time
to contemplate the light.

You count your blessings.
The evening beats its low tattoo.
You hold your breath. You breathe
again. Every year has two

beginnings.

Gate

There's no track of a hedge,
no trace of a fence.
In the middle of a field
an iron gate and no evidence

of path or passage.
It clings to rusty hinges
on chiselled stone,
it hardly infringes

on the course of stock –
for cattle a pair
of scratching posts,
for the colt and chestnut mare

a nuzzling place where you pause
and again you contemplate
in the middle of open grazing
your fate

by a gate that stops nothing
and points nowhere . . .
Say for a moment
the field is your

life and you come
to a gate at the centre
of it. What then?
Then you pause. And open it. And enter.

KERRY HARDIE

Why did I choose these poems? When the initial request came in, they seemed to select themselves quite spontaneously, but now I can barely remember the rationale behind the choice. I suppose I see "Avatar" as a clean poem. It came in a way that surprised me, and said exactly what I wanted to say. I like the cold, fresh wind blowing through it. I also like the fact that when I read it people sometimes hear the word "abattoir" instead of "avatar". Once a poet came up to me afterwards and said when he'd heard the title he'd expected rivers of blood, but none came. . . .

"Exiles" was a cumulative poem that took me a long time to complete. I wanted to write about exile in a general way, but also to tell my mother-in-law's historical story and to record her exile-from-herself through Alzheimer's. When Nancy, the shepherd's wife in the poem, told me her grandfather's history, I had an extraordinarily strong feeling that the poignancy of these forgotten lives should be acknowledged.

"When Maura Had Died" is a "credo" poem for me, especially the last verse. It emerged from a deep respect for the conduct of Maura's partner through that last illness, and from grief for her death when it came. It was written inside that strange, empty space that follows death: when nothing matters and everything matters – both at the same time. "Derrynane '05" is essentially a place poem that records a beloved landscape but also acknowledges the change and uncertainty behind all things. Once I had selected this poem it was natural also to choose "The High Pyrenees", which is essentially about the certainty behind this uncertainty.

Avatar

Listen, this is the trinity, he said, tramping the wet road
in the thin well-being of a winter morning:
God the curlew, God the eider, God the cheese-on-toast.
To his right a huddle of small blue mountains
squatted together discussing the recent storm.
To his left the sea washed.

I thought it was whimsical, what he said,
I condemned it as fey.
Then I saw that he meant it; that, unlike me, he had
        no quarrel
with himself, could see his own glory
was young enough for faith still in flesh and in being.
He was not attracted by awe

or a high cold cleanness
but imagined a god as intimate
as the trickles of blood and juice that coursed about
        inside him,
a god he could eat or warm his hands on,
a low god for winter:
belly-weighted, with the unmistakable call
of the bog curlew or the sea-going eider.

Exiles

1

This is a work of remembrance, the remembrance of lives.
And of times. Of land, water, sky.
Sometimes there are only the names and the lives are lost;
sometimes there are only the lives and the names are lost.
To remember, in a time of forgetting.
I was standing on spread newspapers,
an altar vase locked under my arm,
my hand's warmth misting its yellow brass,
pulling at the flowers in it, stiff and still fresh,
although it was ten days from Christmas –
and Nancy, beside me in the frozen church, saying she had
    Irish in her.

They came away in a mass, their stems embedded,
I had to stamp on them to break the ice
to free out ivy that I wanted for the funeral vases.

My mother-in-law was coming in her coffin
to lie in the stone-dark through the Northern night.
And none of us minded that –
not the coldness nor the sweep of the wind –
because she'd always liked outside, all-weather,
and the next day she would move off, we would follow after
to stand while she took the place prepared for her
in the slit earth in the grey bowl of the hills.

Nancy said it was her father that had made her love
    the music.
Her father was half-Irish; his father had been Irish.
She was trying to make me understand
But I was thinking of flowers
and I didn't. *My father was illegitimate.*
The hardness of the old word focused me.
Her grandfather's name – Sheridan – was on the
    Certificate.
He had come here, but she didn't know why.
Then he had gone away again.

No, she answered me, he hadn't let her down.
He would have married her, her people wouldn't have
    him.
They sent him off. But they kept his child.

Nancy was telling me this, her eyes bright, fresh,
everything direct, her voice lifting, falling with the
    Northern vowels,
her face young, and there was nothing ever that need be
    hidden

Or avoided. She was a shepherd's wife, for forty years
they'd kept a farm on the high moors,
had watched the weather build over Scotland,
the rim of light edging the rise of the land,
the clean rain hanging from the pointed grasses.

She hadn't known my mother-in-law to talk to, only by
    sight.
I thought to say to Nancy, she was Irish too,
although she had the accent of an English lady;
I nearly said it but I didn't,
I wanted to leave Nancy with her Irish grandfather
who had come there and gone away again,
whose name had been Sheridan,
who was likely as not a labourer or a drover.

2

At my feet were florist's bunches:
tiger lilies, spray chrysanthemums.
I wanted holly for its shiny darkness,
so I could drown the florist's flowers in it,
so I could take her back to her beginnings,
which was where she had taken herself through the
    Alzheimer's.
I wanted her to lie there in the frozen darkness,
    unharassed by tiger lilies or chrysanthemums.
My husband, her youngest son, went out into the fading
    light
and cut long spears of holly from the churchyard,
and I broke the stems and thrust them
into the mouths of the vases, brassy as cymbals.

And Nancy said to leave the spent flowers and the bits of stem
because it was her turn for cleaning and she loved the music –
the fiddles and the pipes. I saw him then, her Irish grand-father,
his back turned, tramping away,
over those bleak moors which pulse with larks in summer.

3

She died in the deep of winter
when the cattle break out of the empty fields
when the earth has split open in darkness
and the white mist pours its breath into the night.

On her coffin, only the name she took when she was
    married.
Gone, all of her life before that ceremonial crossing,
all her crowded ancestors are shooed away,
no point them to come peering

over the rim of the darkness like so many gargoyles,
they'll get no satisfaction here, nor any welcome.
Nor would she have wanted them in her lucid days,
but after things started colliding and sliding away
the landscape was all changed and changed
and even her husband of sixty years didn't know its
    contours.
None could say where she roamed nor whom she lived
    with.
All we were sure of was it was not us.

4

In Ireland a man must have a home town,
somewhere to leave behind him, somewhere to long to
    return to.
A woman makes her home town in her children.
In them she makes her claim, in them is her
    belonging.

Shelagh Jacob was her name.
She has gone into the dark with all the rest of them
and it is "Nobody's funeral, for there is no one to bury".
Ah, but there is, there's a husk in a box and all us live
    ones
waiting to bear witness to a womb
that spewed new generations for the dark.

He, leaving his name, losing his child
She, losing her name, leaving children.
And what she liked and what she didn't like
is only personality. And the live children that she
    bore
are only issue. Her one dead child
is only suffering. And there is nothing to lose
for it is all already gone.

We stand in the frozen grass;
the skeins of geese fly over –
dissolving, reforming,
thinning out like stitches on leather,
bunching close, like strung beads.

6

The flight home was delayed and we waited, bone tired. I
thought of Dublin and the long drive home through the
softer, darker Irish night; of how in the morning we would
wake in our own place with its small blue mountains and its
tangled fields, far from this country of moors and high fells
and rapid broken streams.
I thought of the man Sheridan, his boots and his stick.

7

And now it is near to the solstice again.
The old man, her husband, is dying
Slowly. The body, taking its time.
And evening after evening, all through the year
after the urgent work, I have sat with this piece,
trying to understand; failing.
And all I have left is remembrance,
frail and wavering as dream.

This is a work of remembrance, the remembrance of lives.
And of times. Of land, water, sky.
Sometimes there are only the names and the lives are lost,
sometimes there are only the lives and the names are lost.
To remember, in a time of forgetting.
In the long wail of the pipes, the language of remembrance,
and Nancy, her clear eyes looking ahead,
her yearning and remembrance in the music.

When Maura Had Died
for Carmel

These days –
        filled with wonder of death.

This morning I woke early,
watched the day come, blue and hard-won,
the rain's clean shine on the glass, the drops
on the crossbar hanging in the light.
I knew dailiness, saw birds
moving across the window, saw the window
for a portal, as in Renaissance painting.

I never knew
that death was this simple;
you left
as a woman holding a letter
moves to the light –

Then I wanted the grace
to share the open secret,
to be wasp in the apple and apple arching
around the devouring wasp,
sheltering its feeding. Oh, let me live living,
devoured and devouring,
eating myself down
to my own core.

Derrynane '05

It was well after seven
but how could we leave?
it would have been
like spitting in the face of God.
A cormorant surfaced and dived,
surfaced and dived, blue shadows
lay down in the scuffled footprints,
the long, glass waves curled over
and broke into spatters of light.

Yellow rattle, eyebright, bedstraw,
sea holly, milkwort.
Nobody there but us.
We stayed on – the pale sand, the evening,
the islands all turning
smoke-blue and floating away –
stayed as we'd done so often before,
but might not again,
the times being frailer,
everything being frailer.
Old ways fall away,
the cormorant's wings beat
black on the water,
the world's going spinning off
to God-knows-where.

The High Pyrenees

I lifted my eyes and there was the sea of the
  mountains,
wave upon wave, and far out on the ocean, white
  peaks,

then the silence came close and stood there beside
  me and waited,
and I knew there was nothing to want or to fear or
  to say —

there was only the ancient sea of the mountains,
only the night coming down on the great dark slide
  of its waves.

SEAMUS HEANEY

Any dictionary will provide more meanings for the word "cast" than you might expect to find. I looked it up when I was asking myself how and why I chose the poems included here. I wanted to start with the old comparison of writing to angling and draw an analogy between the way a poem gets written and the way a choice like this gets made, because there is a similarity between the casting about for something decided which characterises the process of composition and the equally provisional, trial-and-error process of list-making that goes into the job in hand here.

In one sense you are making a cast list, choosing a group of performers who will go out there and do their thing and not disgrace themselves or you. In another you are – as with lots – drawing or choosing in full awareness that there will always be something random about the final outcome. One thing, however, will be certain in all cases: the poems you choose will be those in which you cast something of yourself, both in the sense of having shaped it and having shed it, as in the casting of metal or the casting of a skin – or an anchor.

The moment I wrote them, each of these five poems felt right because each in their different way, at different periods, provided that double sensation of having formulated some anxiety or apprehension or intuition and at the same time freed it up. They had the fluency and the fixity of a shadow cast by someone on the move through a life. Or maybe I just see it that way because of the cast in my eye.

The Tollund Man

I

Some day I will go to Aarhus
To see his peat-brown head,
The mild pods of his eye-lids,
His pointed skin cap.

In the flat country nearby
Where they dug him out,
His last gruel of winter seeds
Caked in his stomach,

Naked except for
The cap, noose and girdle,
I will stand a long time.
Bridegroom to the goddess,

She tightened her torc on him
And opened her fen,
Those dark juices working
Him to a saint's kept body,

Trove of the turfcutters'
Honeycombed workings.
Now his stained face
Reposes at Aarhus.

II

I could risk blasphemy,
Consecrate the cauldron bog
Our holy ground and pray
Him to make germinate

The scattered, ambushed
Flesh of labourers,
Stockinged corpses
Laid out in the farmyards,

Tell-tale skin and teeth
Flecking the sleepers
Of four young brothers, trailed
For miles along the lines.

III

Something of his sad freedom
As he rode the tumbril
Should come to me, driving,
Saying the names

Tollund, Grauballe, Nebelgard,
Watching the pointing hands
Of country people,
Not knowing their tongue.

Out there in Jutland
In the old man-killing parishes
I will feel lost,
Unhappy and at home.

Casualty

I

He would drink by himself
And raise a weathered thumb
Towards the high shelf,
Calling another rum
And blackcurrant, without
Having to raise his voice,
Or order a quick stout
By a lifting of the eyes
And a discreet dumb-show
Of pulling off the top;
At closing time would go
In waders and peaked cap
Into the showery dark,
A dole-kept breadwinner
But a natural for work.
I loved his whole manner,
Sure-footed but too sly,
His deadpan sidling tact,
His fisherman's quick eye
And turned observant back.

Incomprehensible
To him, my other life.
Sometimes on his high stool,
Too busy with his knife

At a tobacco plug
And not meeting my eye,
In the pause after a slug
He mentioned poetry.
We would be on our own
And, always politic
And shy of condescension,
I would manage by some trick
To switch the talk to eels
Or lore of the horse and cart
Or the Provisionals.

But my tentative art
His turned back watches too:
He was blown to bits
Out drinking in a curfew
Others obeyed, three nights
After they shot dead
The thirteen men in Derry.
PARAS THIRTEEN, the walls said,
BOGSIDE NIL. That Wednesday
Everyone held
His breath and trembled.

II

It was a day of cold
Raw silence, wind-blown
Surplice and soutane:
Rained-on, flower-laden
Coffin after coffin
Seemed to float from the door
Of the packed cathedral
Like blossoms on slow water.
The common funeral
Unrolled its swaddling band,
Lapping, tightening
Till we were braced and bound
Like brothers in a ring.

But he would not be held
At home by his own crowd
Whatever threats were phoned,
Whatever black flags waved.
I see him as he turned
In that bombed offending place,
Remorse fused with terror
In his still knowable face,
His cornered outfaced stare
Blinding in the flash.

He had gone miles away
For he drank like a fish
Nightly, naturally
Swimming towards the lure
Of warm lit-up places,
The blurred mesh and murmur
Drifting among glasses
In the gregarious smoke.
How culpable was he
That last night when he broke
Our tribe's complicity?
"Now, you're supposed to be
An educated man,"
I hear him say. "Puzzle me
The right answer to that one."

III

I missed his funeral,
Those quiet walkers
And sideways talkers
Shoaling out of his lane
To the respectable
Purring of the hearse . . .
They move in equal pace
With the habitual
Slow consolation
Of a dawdling engine,

The line lifted, hand
Over fist, cold sunshine
On the water, the land
Banked under fog: that morning
When he took me in his boat,
The screw purling, turning
Indolent fathoms white,
I tasted freedom with him.
To get out early, haul
Steadily off the bottom,
Dispraise the catch, and smile
As you find a rhythm
Working you, slow mile by mile,
Into your proper haunt
Somewhere, well out, beyond . . .

Dawn-sniffing revenant,
Plodder through midnight rain,
Question me again.

The Harvest Bow

As you plaited the harvest bow
You implicated the mellowed silence in you
In wheat that does not rust
But brightens as it tightens twist by twist
Into a knowable corona,
A throwaway love-knot of straw.

Hands that aged round ashplants and cane sticks
And lapped the spurs on a lifetime of game cocks
Harked to their gift and worked with fine intent
Until your fingers moved somnambulant:
I tell and finger it like braille,
Gleaning the unsaid off the palpable,

And if I spy into its golden loops
I see us walk between the railway slopes
Into an evening of long grass and midges,
Blue smoke straight up, old beds and ploughs in hedges,
An auction notice on an outhouse wall –
You with a harvest bow in your lapel,

Me with the fishing rod, already homesick
For the big lift of these evenings, as your stick
Whacking the tips off weeds and bushes
Beats out of time, and beats, but flushes
Nothing: that original townland
Still tongue-tied in the straw tied by your hand.

The end of art is peace
Could be the motto of this frail device
That I have pinned up on our deal dresser –
Like a drawn snare
Slipped lately by the spirit of the corn
Yet burnished by its passage, and still warm.

A Sofa in the Forties

All of us on the sofa in a line, kneeling
Behind each other, eldest down to youngest,
Elbows going like pistons, for this was a train

And between the jamb-wall and the bedroom door
Our speed and distance were inestimable.
First we shunted, then we whistled, then

Somebody collected the invisible
For tickets and very gravely punched it
As carriage after carriage under us

Moved faster, *chooka-chook*, the sofa legs
Went giddy and the unreachable ones
Far out on the kitchen floor began to wave.

*

Ghost-train? Death-gondola? The carved, curved ends,
Black leatherette and ornate gauntness of it
Made it seem the sofa had achieved

Flotation. Its castors on tip-toe,
Its braid and fluent backboard gave it airs
Of superannuated pageantry:

When visitors endured it, straight-backed,
When it stood off in its own remoteness,
When the insufficient toys appeared on it

On Christmas mornings, it held out as itself,
Potentially heavenbound, earthbound for sure,
Among things that might add up or let you down

*

We entered history and ignorance
Under the wireless shelf. *Yippee-i-ay,*
Sang "The Riders of the Range". HERE IS THE NEWS,

Said the absolute speaker. Between him and us
A great gulf was fixed where pronunciation
Reigned tyrannically. The aerial wire

Swept from a treetop down in through a hole
Bored in the windowframe. When it moved in wind,
The sway of language and its furtherings

Swept and swayed in us like nets in water
Or the abstract, lonely curve of distant trains
As we entered history and ignorance.

*

We occupied our seats with all our might,
Fit for the uncomfortableness.
Constancy was its own reward already.

Out in front, on the big upholstered arm,
Somebody craned to the side, driver or
Fireman, wiping his dry brow with the air

Of one who had run the gauntlet. We were
The last thing on his mind, it seemed; we sensed
A tunnel coming up where we'd pour through

Like unlit carriages through fields at night,
Our only job to sit, eyes straight ahead,
And be transported and make engine noise.

The Blackbird of Glanmore

On the grass when I arrive,
Filling the stillness with life,
But ready to scare off
At the very first wrong move,
In the ivy when I leave.

It's you, blackbird, I love.

I park, pause, take heed.
Breathe. Just breathe and sit
And lines I once translated
Come back: "I want away
To the house of death, to my father

Under the low clay roof."

And I think of one gone to him,
A little stillness dancer –
Haunter-son, lost brother –
Cavorting through the yard,
So glad to see me home,

My homesick first term over.

And think of a neighbour's words
Long after the accident:
"Yon bird on the shed roof,
Up on the ridge for weeks –
I said nothing at the time

But I never liked yon bird."

The automatic lock
Clunks shut, the blackbird's panic
Is shortlived, for a second
I've a bird's eye view of myself,
A shadow on raked gravel

In front of my house of life.

Hedge-hop, I am absolute
For you, your ready talkback,
Your each stand-offish comeback,
Your picky, nervy goldbeak –
On the grass when I arrive,

In the ivy when I leave.

RITA ANN HIGGINS

These were the only new poems I had when asked
to contribute to this anthology.

Ciontach

Bhí mé óg
bhí eagla orm faoi gach rúd
bhí na hirisí ag teacht:

"The Far East"
"The Irish Messenger of the Sacred Heart"

agus an chuid eile acu.
bhí mé ceathar nó cúig bliain d'aois
bhí na hirisí ag teacht
bhí gach daoine í mo theach ag dul chuig an bhfaoistin
ag dul ar Aifreann
bhí brón ar gach duine.
Duirt siad le Dia
tá bhrón orainn a Dhia,
bhí mé óg
bhí brón orm freisin.
Dúirt mé le Dia
tá brón orm a Dhia
bhí rud éigein ag tarlú
bhí na h-irisí ag teacht
bhí arán agus subh go flúirseach sa teach

Guilty

(translated by Rita Ann Higgins)

I was young
I was afraid of everything
the magazines were coming:

"The Far East"
"The Irish Messenger of the Sacred Heart"

and the rest of them.
I was four or five years old
the magazines were coming
everyone in the house was going to confession
going to mass
everyone was sad.
They said to God
we are sad God.
I was young
I was sad too.
I said to God
I'm sad God.
Something was happening
the magazines were coming
bread and jam was plentiful in the house

bhí na hirisí go flúirseach
bhí eagla orm faoi gach rud
bhí mé ciontach
bhí na cearca ciontach
bhí na madraí ciontach
bhí na clocha ciontach
bhí an líne i lár an bhóthair ciontach
bhí an tobar ciontach:
d'ól muid as
bhí muid go léir ciontach.

the magazines were plentiful
I was afraid of everything
I was guilty
the hens were guilty
the dogs were guilty
the stones were guilty
the line in the middle of the road was guilty
the well was guilty:
we drank from it
we were all guilty.

The Immortals

The boy racers quicken on the Spiddal road
in Barbie Pink souped-ups
or roulette red Honda Civics,
with few fault lines or face lifts to rev up about
only an unwritten come hither of thrills
with screeching propositions and no full stops –
if you are willing to ride the ride.

Hop you in filly in my passion wagon.
Loud music and cigarette butts are shafted into space.
We'll speed hump it all the way baby
look at me, look at me
I'm young, I'm immortal, I'm free.

Gemmas and Emmas
stick insects or supermodels
regulars at "Be a Diva"
for the perfect nails
eyebrows to slice bread with
and landing strips to match.

They wear short lives
they dream of never slowing down-pours
while half syllable after half syllable
jerk from their peak capped idols' lips.
Their skinny lovers melt into seats
made for bigger men
Look at me, look at me
I'm young, I'm immortal, I'm free.
The boy racers never grow older or fatter.

On headstones made from Italian marble
they become "our loving son Keith"
"our beloved son Jonathan", etcetera etcetera.
On the Spiddal road
itching to pass out the light
they become Zeus, Eros, Vulcan, Somnus.

Dirty Dancer

In the Tai Chi garden
in Hong Kong
an old man –
the only smoker there
flicks through a porno magazine.
He has a huge wart on his lip.

His laidback, scratch my arse,
bite me look says to anyone
who wants to read it.

Better to be in the park with porn
than four-walling it on the 80th floor
the icicles of lonely
jerking at my heels.

The Darkness

It was Christmas
It was perjury lights
It was anniversary masses
It was death by devotion
It was hospice talk
It was doctor only cards
It was clamping
It was hailstones
It was gallstones
It was jackstones
It was complex stuffing
It was the dishcloth dreams
It was refuse charges
It was soap operas
It was pope operas
It was Spiddal in the middle
It was rain rain rain
It was old wounds
It was open wounds
It was Neven Henaff
It was dirty cups
It was Irish Nazis
It was jagged emotions.
The absence of pheasants

the bareness of trees.
It was icy fog
It was virus after virus
It was Célestin Lainé
It was night classes
It was boy racers
It was dreams in cold places
It was cemetery Sunday
It was mimicry Sunday
It was any Sunday
It was how are u texts
It was ex
It was pect
It was ations
It was keep out the light classes
It was mobile bones
It was broken storage heaters
It was metres and litres.
A season for grieving
the absence of cinnamon
the presence of radon.
It was high cholesterol
It was my cholesterol
It was never me.

Borders

There's no hope of a joy rider here
no front walls, no fences with menaces
no Rottweilers, no child eating Dobermans
no pinch of tension in the air
that sets fire to a good night's sleep
no jumpiness that incites the joints
to early arthritis.

This is pheasantville
easy peasy, boreen and bog
warbler boulevard
meander lane the pace the same
the borders here are invisible
you'll find them rarely in the bend of a look
the vexed angle of a grin
the crew cut greeting,
the verb that takes longer to pall.

Brendan Kennelly

I'm just back from America and got your warm letter. Thank you, John. I'd love to contribute to that exciting book and am honoured that you invited me. I'll give you a reason or two for my choices.

"God's Eye": This, because I've always loved birds since I was a child, and the idea that God's eye (the sun) gives them, and us, the light they and we need to see each other in so many different states (terror of the birds in this instance after my father clapped his hands) still fascinates me. Birds themselves are among the most striking of nature's beauties and terrorists.

"Eily Kilbride": Although the poem is set in Cork, it could be any city in Ireland. Despite the Celtic Tiger and "success", children beg in the streets of Dublin; many families are ripped apart by drugs and a new, ravaging poverty; innocence is often a tearful child in a begging doorway.

"Poem from a Three Year Old": Here is the true beauty of childhood, or a good part of it, anyway: passionately asking questions and at the same time wanting to have fun, to play, to shake off the darkness of asking questions about death. Having fun, asking questions. After forty-two years as a teacher, I think these two elements are at the heart of education. I love learning from children.

"Yes": This poem is about one of the deepest battles in many people, certainly in me: that conflict, that battle between yes and no, light and dark, positivism and negativism, good and evil, and so many other forces. It is a poem about choice, about deliberations, about stopping at endless emotional and spiritual crossroads. I believe it is especially pertinent today. But it has always been in me.

"Begin": This is probably the most simple poem of the five, yet I know it has helped people in sickness, in marriage break-ups, in deep personal problematic, even tragic, situations. It is a poem re-written from many years ago. This re-writing came after a heart operation (which also produced *The Man Made of Rain*). To be quite frank and honest, if a poem of mine helps others (as this "Begin" strangely helped me), I simply love to make that poem available to people in need. And I think there is a fundamental, essential, enduring truth in the lines.

So that's my choice, John. I could suggest others, but I like the sense of connection between these five poems.

God's Eye

Beneath the stare of God's gold burning eye,
Two crisp hands clap; a thousand plover rise
And wheel across the clean meadows of the sky.

Black wings flash and gleam; a perfect white
Makes beautiful each rising breast,
Sovereign in the far-off miracle of flight.

Their terror is a lovely thing,
A sudden inspiration, exploding
In the thunder of each beating wing;

A startling rout, as of an army driven
In broken regiments
Against the proud, fantastic face of heaven.

And yet, no mad disorder, no raucous accident
Deforms the miracle; high flocks
Fulfil an inbred, furious intent.

In screams of dread, perfection whirls
Along the headlands of the sky;
They circle, gabbing now like girls,

And wing to safety in Carrig Wood,
Dip through branches, disappear; across the sky,
The pale sun throws a quilt of solitude.

After terror, they are safety's prisoners,
Momentary victims of security
In labyrinths where surly winter stirs.

They breathe on branches, hidden and alone.
Fear will flare again, but now the abandoned sky
Is turning cold and grey as stone.

I think about that marvellous rout, the empty sky,
A flight of plover hidden from
The stare of God's gold burning eye.

Eily Kilbride

On the North side of Cork city
Where I sported and played
On the banks of my own lovely Lee
Having seen the goat break loose in Grand Parade

I met a child, Eily Kilbride
Who'd never heard of marmalade,
Whose experience of breakfast
Was coldly limited,

Whose entire school day
Was a bag of crisps,
Whose parents had no work to do,

Who went, once, into the countryside,
Saw a horse with a feeding bag over its head
And thought it was sniffing glue.

Poem from a Three Year Old

And will the flowers die?

And will the people die?

And every day do you grow old, do I
grow old, no I'm not old, do
flowers grow old?

Old things – do you throw them out?

Do you throw old people out?

And how you know a flower that's old?

The petals fall, the petals fall from flowers,
and do the petals fall from people too,
every day more petals fall until the
floor where I would like to play I
want to play is covered with old
flowers and people all the same
together lying there with petals fallen
on the dirty floor I want to play
the floor you come and sweep
with the huge broom.

The dirt you sweep, what happens that
what happens all the dirt you sweep
from flowers and people, what
happens all the dirt? Is all the

dirt what's left of flowers
and people, all the dirt there in a
heap under the huge broom that
sweeps everything away?

Why you work so hard, why brush
and sweep to make a heap of dirt?
And who will bring new flowers?
And who will bring new people? Who will
bring new flowers to put in water
where no petals fall on to the
floor where I would like to
play? Who will bring new flowers
that will not hang their heads

like tired old people wanting sleep?
Who will bring new flowers that
do not split and shrivel every
day? And if we have new flowers,
will we have new people too to
keep the flowers alive and give
them water?

And will the new young flowers die?

And will the new young people die?

And why?

Yes

I love the word
And hear its long struggle with no
Even in the bird's throat
And the budging crocus.
Some winter's night
I see it flood the faces
Of my friends, ripen their laughter
And plant early flowers in
Their conversation.

You will understand when I say
It is for me a morning word
Though it is older than the sea
And hisses in a way
That may have given
An example
To the serpent itself.
It is this ageless incipience
Whose influence is found
In the first and last pages of books,
In the grim skin of the affirmative battler
And in the voices of women
That constitutes the morning quality
Of yes.

We have all
Thought what it must be like
Never to grow old,
The dreams of our elders have mythic endurance
Though their hearts are stilled
But the only agelessness
Is yes.

I am always beginning to appreciate
The agony from which it is born.
Clues from here and there
Suggest such agony is hard to bear
But is the shaping God
Of the word that we
Sometimes hear, and struggle to be.

Begin

Begin again to the summoning birds
to the sight of light at the window,
begin to the roar of morning traffic
all along Pembroke Road.
Every beginning is a promise
born in light and dying in dark
determination and exaltation of springtime
flowering the way to work.
Begin to the pageant of queuing girls
the arrogant loneliness of swans in the canal
bridges linking the past and future
old friends passing though with us still.
Begin to the loneliness that cannot end
since it perhaps is what makes us begin,
begin to wonder at unknown faces
at crying birds in the sudden rain
at branches stark in the willing sunlight
at seagulls foraging for bread
at couples sharing a sunny secret
alone together while making good.
Though we live in a world that dreams of ending
that always seems about to give in
something that will not acknowledge conclusion
insists that we forever begin.

MICHAEL LONGLEY

These five poems took me by surprise and, in a way, still do.

I wrote "The Linen Industry" in 1977 when my younger daughter was still a toddler. Sarah kept crawling over me on the sofa, but the love poem insisted on being born, arranging itself quite naturally into quatrains. For me there has always been something magical about six quatrains, twenty-four lines. Why do so many poems fall into this shape? Love poetry is at the core of the enterprise.

In the summer of 1994 there were rumours of an IRA ceasefire. At the time I was reading the passage in the Iliad where Priam the old Trojan king visits the tent of the great Greek general Achilles to beg for the corpse of his son Hector whom Achilles has killed in combat. I wanted to compress this episode into a short poem and perhaps make my own minuscule contribution to the peace process. On the train from Dublin to Belfast I suddenly realised that if I were to put Priam's first action at the end of the poem, I would have a rhyming couplet and the makings of a sonnet. When I got home, "Ceasefire" seemed to write itself.

In April 1989 I was sitting at my boss's desk in the Arts Council going over budgets with him when Section VIII of "Ghetto" came into my mind. Pretending to take down financial notes, I scribbled a draft. Section I came a month later. I did not envisage a sequence. Indeed, it was a whole year before the remaining six sections haphazardly presented themselves. How can we write about the abomination of the Holocaust? I showed "Ghetto" to my friend, the dancer and choreographer Helen Lewis, who is an Auschwitz survivor. Only when she approved did I feel free to publish.

I have spent some of my happiest days in my friend Ronald Ewart's old house in Cardoso, a small hill-top village in Tuscany. Though gathered from the immediate environment, the images in "Etruria" are meant to carry deeper historical resonances.

Likewise, in "The Leveret" my grandson's first visit to Carrigskeewaun sparked off a sense of family history and also suggested how the human family belongs to the natural world, its nurturing and dangers. The great Irish ornithologist David Cabot has for nearly forty years allowed me to stay in his cottage in the remote Mayo townland of Carrigskeewaun. At least a third of my poems have been conceived there.

The Linen Industry

Pulling up flax after the blue flowers have fallen
And laying our handfuls in the peaty water
To rot those grasses to the bone, or building stooks
That recall the skirts of an invisible dancer,

We become a part of the linen industry
And follow its processes to the grubby town
Where fields are compacted into window-boxes
And there is little room among the big machines.

But even in our attic under the skylight
We make love on a bleach green, the whole meadow
Draped with material turning white in the sun
As though snow reluctant to melt were our attire.

What's passion but a battering of stubborn stalks,
Then a gentle combing out of fibres like hair
And a weaving of these into christening robes,
Into garments for a marriage or funeral?

Since it's like a bereavement once the labour's done
To find ourselves last workers in a dying trade,
Let flax be our matchmaker, our undertaker,
The provider of sheets for whatever the bed –

And be shy of your breasts in the presence of death,
Say that you look more beautiful in linen
Wearing white petticoats, the bow on your bodice
A butterfly attending the embroidered flowers.

Ceasefire

I

Put in mind of his own father and moved to tears
Achilles took him by the hand and pushed the old king
Gently away, but Priam curled up at his feet and
Wept with him until their sadness filled the building.

II

Taking Hector's corpse into his own hands Achilles
Made sure it was washed and, for the old king's sake,
Laid out in uniform, ready for Priam to carry
Wrapped like a present home to Troy at daybreak.

III

When they had eaten together, it pleased them both
To stare at each other's beauty as lovers might,
Achilles built like a god, Priam good-looking still
And full of conversation, who earlier had sighed:

IV

"I get down on my knees and do what must be done
And kiss Achilles' hand, the killer of my son."

Ghetto

I

Because you will suffer soon and die, your choices
Are neither right nor wrong: a spoon will feed you,
A flannel keep you clean, a toothbrush bring you back
To your bathroom's view of chimney-pots and gardens.
With so little time for inventory or leavetaking,
You are packing now for the rest of your life
Photographs, medicines, a change of underwear, a book,
A candlestick, a loaf, sardines, needle and thread.
These are your heirlooms, perishables, worldly goods.
What you bring is the same as what you leave behind,
Your last belonging a list of your belongings.

II

As though it were against the law to sleep on pillows
They have filled a cathedral with confiscated feathers:
Silence irrefrangible, no room for angels' wings,
Tons of feathers suffocating cherubim and seraphim.

III

The little girl without a mother behaves like a mother
With her rag doll to whom she explains fear and anguish,
The meagreness of the bread ration, how to make it last,

How to get back to the doll's house and lift up the roof
And, before the flame-throwers and dynamiters destroy it,
How to rescue from their separate rooms love and sorrow,
Masterpieces the size of a postage stamp, small fortunes.

IV

From among the hundreds of thousands I can imagine one
Behind the barbed-wire fences as my train crosses Poland.
I see him for long enough to catch the sprinkle of snowflakes
On his hair and schoolbag, and then I am transported
Away from that world of broken hobby-horses and silent toys.
He turns into a little snowman and refuses to melt.

V

For street-singers in the marketplace, weavers, warp-makers,
Those who suffer in sewing-machine repair shops, excrement
Removal workers, there are not enough root vegetables,
Beetroots, turnips, swedes, nor for the leather-stitchers
Who are boiling leather so that their children may eat;
Who are turning like a thick slice of potato-bread
This page, which is everything I know about potatoes,
My delivery of Irish Peace, Beauty of Hebron, Home
Guard, Arran Banners, Kerr's Pinks, resistant to eelworm,
Resignation, common scab, terror, frost, potato-blight.

VI

There will be performances in the waiting room, and time
To jump over a skipping rope, and time to adjust
As though for a dancing class the ribbons in your hair.
This string quartet is the most natural thing in the world.

VII

Fingers leave shadows on a violin, harmonics,
A blackbird fluttering between electrified fences.

VIII

Lessons were forbidden in that terrible school.
Punishable by death were reading and writing
And arithmetic, so that even the junior infants
Grew old and wise in lofts studying these subjects.
There were drawing lessons, and drawings of kitchens
And farms, farm animals, butterflies, mothers, fathers
Who survived in crayon until in pen and ink
They turned into guards at executions and funerals
Torturing and hanging even these stick figures.
There were drawings of barracks and latrines as well
And the only windows were the windows they drew.

Etruria

Pavese's English poems, an English setter barking –
Too hot and clammy to read, sleep, dander, so
Snap my walking stick in two and lay it out beside
My long bones in an ossuary that tells a story,

The apprentice ivory carver's yarn, for instance,
Who etched those elderly twinkling Chinese pilgrims
On a walnut, shell-crinkles their only obstacle,
Globe-trotters in my palm, the kernel still rattling.

You can find me under the sellotaped map fold
Stuck with dog hairs, and close to a mulberry bush
The women tended, coddling between their breasts
The silkworms' filaments, vulnerable bobbins.

Was it a humming bird or a humming bird moth
Mistook my navel for some chubby convolvulus?
Paolo steps from his *casa* like an astronaut
And stoops with smoky bellows among his bees.

Gin, acacia honey, last year's sloes, crimson
Slipping its gravity like the satellite that swims
In and out of the hanging hornet-traps, then
Jukes between midnight planes and shooting stars.

The trout that dozed in a perfect circle wear
Prison grey in the fridge, bellies sky-coloured
Next to the butter dish's pattern, traveller's joy,
Old man's beard when it seeds, feathery plumes.

The melon Adua leaves me on the windowsill
Gift-wrapped in a paper bag and moonlight,
Ripens in moon-breezes, the pipistrelle's whooshes,
My own breathing and the insomniac aspen's.

A liver concocted out of darkness and wine
Dregs, the vinegar mother sulking in her crock
Haruspicates fever, shrivelled grapes, vipers
On the footpath to a non-existent waterfall.

I escape the amorous mongrel with dewclaws
And vanish where once the privy stood, my kaftan
Snagging on the spiral staircase down to the small
Hours when house and I get into bed together,

My mattress on the floor, crickets, scorpion shapes
In their moonlit square, my space in this cellar
Beneath old rafters and old stones, Etruria,
Nightmare's cesspit, the mosquito-buzz of sleep.

The Leveret

for my grandson, Benjamin

This is your first night in Carrigskeewaun.
The Owennadornaun is so full of rain
You arrived in Paddy Morrison's tractor,
A bumpy approach in your father's arms
To the cottage where, all of one year ago,
You were conceived, a fire-seed in the hearth.
Did you hear the wind in the fluffy chimney?
Do you hear the wind tonight, and the rain
And a shore bird calling from the mussel reefs?
Tomorrow I'll introduce you to the sea,
Little hoplite. Have you been missing it?
I'll park your chariot by the otters' rock
And carry you over seaweed to the sea.
There's a tufted duck on David's lake
With her sootfall of hatchlings, pompoms
A day old and already learning to dive.
We may meet the stoat near the erratic
Boulder, a shrew in his mouth, or the merlin
Meadow-pipit-hunting. But don't be afraid.
The leveret breakfasts under the fuchsia
Every morning, and we shall be watching.
I have picked wild flowers for you, scabious
And centaury in a jam jar of water
That will bend and magnify the daylight.
This is your first night in Carrigskeewaun.

Derek Mahon

I've chosen these poems because they've survived long enough, in my own view, for me to be sure I like or at least tolerate them. This even goes for the "Shed", a grandiose bit of rhetoric I like less than the "Garage", also grandiose but somehow less annoyingly so, I think. "An Unborn Child" because it's one of my earliest. "Shapes and Shadows" because it's two kinds of poems in one, both treating typical subject-matter: the North, and Art. "Roman Script", ten years old, is far enough away for me to see it objectively but recent enough to count as (almost) up-to-date. These cover a period of near-enough forty years.

When the late Katharine Washburn included me in a big Norton book of world poetry, she shrewdly chose the unborn child rather than the disused shed, finding it closer to human experience, I suspect, and I think it still stands up after all these years. The "child" is probably the poet himself looking forward to grown-up life and then sharing a dark-into-light storyline and so on, but it's hard for a perpetrator to get a perspective on his own work, thematically at least. No consistent theme is evident to me; but the formal picture is obvious enough. The writer is clearly a prisoner of the iambic pentameter and, worse, a slave to rhyme, yet his rhymes are trite, as if he doesn't really think them an important feature. Why does he do this? He's done other things too, but he always comes back to the same old tune, even after forty years. Blame his miseducation.

"Roman Script" was deliberately constructed to commemorate a happy time in that city where everything looks like a film set. We visited Hugh O'Neill's grave; also the house where he and his retinue lived in their exile. Once church property, the Palazzo dei Penitenzieri is now the Hotel Columbus, its slogan: "Scoperta un Nuovo Mondo!" Discover a new world!

An Unborn Child

for Michael and Edna Longley

I have already come to the verge of
Departure; a month or so and
I shall be vacating this familiar room.
Its fabric fits me almost like a glove
While leaving latitude for a free hand.
I begin to put on the manners of the world
Sensing the splitting light above
My head, where in the silence I lie curled.

Certain mysteries are relayed to me
Through the dark network of my mother's body
While she sits sewing the white shrouds
Of my apotheosis. I know the twisted
Kitten that lies there sunning itself
Under the bare bulb, the clouds
Of goldfish mooning around upon the shelf.
In me these data are already vested;

I know them in my bones – bones which embrace
Nothing, for I am completely egocentric.
The pandemonium of encumbrances
Which will absorb me, mind and senses,
Intricacies of the maze and the rat-race,
I imagine only. Though they linger and,
Like fingers, stretch until the knuckles crack,
They cannot dwarf the dimensions of my hand.

I must compose myself at the nerve centre
Of this metropolis, and not fidget –
Although sometimes at night, when the city
Has gone to sleep, I keep in touch with it,
Listening to the warm red water
Racing in the sewers of my mother's body;
Or the moths, soft as eyelids, or the rain
Wiping its wet wings on the window-pane.

And sometimes too, in the small hours of the morning
When the dead filament has ceased to ring,
After the goldfish are dissolved in darkness
And the kitten has gathered itself up into a ball
Between the groceries and the sewing,
I slip the trappings of my harness
To range these hollows in discreet rehearsal
And, battering at the concavity of my caul,

Produce in my mouth the words, "I want to live!" –
This my first protest, and shall be my last.
As I am innocent, everything I do
Or say is couched in the affirmative.
I want to see, hear, touch and taste
These things with which I am to be encumbered.
Perhaps I needn't worry; give
Or take a day or two, my days are numbered.

A Disused Shed in Co. Wexford

Let them not forget us, the weak souls among the asphodels.
— SEFERIS, *Mythistorema*

for J. G. Farrell

Even now there are places where a thought might grow —
Peruvian mines, worked out and abandoned
To a slow clock of condensation,
An echo trapped for ever, and a flutter
Of wildflowers in the lift-shaft,
Indian compounds where the wind dances
And a door bangs with diminished confidence,
Lime crevices behind rippling rain-barrels,
Dog corners for bone burials;
And in a disused shed in County Wexford,

Deep in the grounds of a burnt-out hotel,
Among the bathtubs and the washbasins
A thousand mushrooms crowd to a keyhole.
This is the one star in their firmament
Or frames a star within a star.
What should they do there but desire?
So many days beyond the rhododendrons
With the world waltzing in its bowl of cloud,
They have learnt patience and silence
Listening to the rooks querulous in the high wood.

They have been waiting for us in a foetor
Of vegetable sweat since civil war days,
Since the gravel-crunching, interminable departure
Of the expropriated mycologist.
He never came back, and light since then
Is a keyhole rusting gently after rain.
Spiders have spun, flies dusted to mildew
And once a day, perhaps, they have heard something –
A trickle of masonry, a shout from the blue
Or a lorry changing gear at the end of the lane.

There have been deaths, the pale flesh flaking
Into the earth that nourished it;
And nightmares, born of these and the grim
Dominion of stale air and rank moisture.
Those nearest the door grow strong –
"Elbow room! Elbow room!"
The rest, dim in a twilight of crumbling
Utensils and broken pitchers, groaning
For their deliverance, have been so long
Expectant that there is left only the posture.

A half century, without visitors, in the dark –
Poor preparation for the cracking lock
And creak of hinges; magi, moonmen,
Powdery prisoners of the old regime,
Web-throated, stalked like triffids, racked by drought

And insomnia, only the ghost of a scream
At the flash-bulb firing-squad we wake them with
Shows there is life yet in their feverish forms.
Grown beyond nature now, soft food for worms,
They lift frail heads in gravity and good faith.

They are begging us, you see, in their wordless way,
To do something, to speak on their behalf
Or at least not to close the door again.
Lost people of Treblinka and Pompeii!
"Save us, save us," they seem to say,
"Let the god not abandon us
Who have come so far in darkness and in pain.
We too had our lives to live.
You with your light meter and relaxed itinerary,
Let not our naive labours have been in vain!"

A Garage in Co. Cork

Surely you paused at this roadside oasis
In your nomadic youth, and saw the mound
Of never-used cement, the curious faces,
The soft-drink ads and the uneven ground
Rainbowed with oily puddles, where a snail
Had scrawled its slimy, phosphorescent trail.

Like a frontier store-front in an old western
It might have nothing behind it but thin air,
Building materials, fruit boxes, scrap iron,
Dust-laden shrubs and coils of rusty wire,
A cabbage-white fluttering in the sodden
Silence of an untended kitchen garden –

Nirvana! But the cracked panes reveal a dark
Interior echoing with the cries of children.
Here in this quiet corner of Co. Cork
A family ate, slept and watched the rain
Dance clean and cobalt the exhausted grit
So that the mind shrank from the glare of it.

Where did they go? South Boston? Cricklewood?
Somebody somewhere thinks of this as home,
Remembering the old pumps where they stood,
Antique now, squirting juice into a cream
Lagonda or a dung-caked tractor while
A cloud swam on a cloud-reflecting tile.

Surely a whitewashed sun-trap at the back
Gave way to hens, wild thyme, and the first few
Shadowy yards of an overgrown cart track,
Tyres in the branches such as Noah knew –
Beyond, a swoop of mountain where you heard,
Disconsolate in the haze, a single blackbird.

Left to itself, the functional will cast
A death-bed glow of picturesque abandon.
The intact antiquities of the recent past,
Dropped from the retail catalogues, return
To the materials that gave rise to them
And shine with a late sacramental gleam.

A god who spent the night here once rewarded
Natural courtesy with eternal life –
Changing to petrol pumps, that they be spared
For ever there, an old man and his wife.
The virgin who escaped his dark design
Sanctions the townland from her prickly shrine.

We might be anywhere but are in one place only,
One of the milestones of earth-residence
Unique in each particular, the thinly
Peopled hinterland serenely tense –
Not in the hope of a resplendent future
But with a sure sense of its intrinsic nature.

"Shapes and Shadows"

– WILLIAM SCOTT, *oil on canvas, Ulster Museum*

The kitchens would grow bright
in blue frames; outside, still
harbour and silent cottages
from a time of shortages,
shapes deft and tranquil,
black kettle and black pot.

Too much the known structures
those simple manufactures,
communion of frying pans,
skinny beans and spoons,
colander and fish-slice
in a polished interior space.

But tension of hand and heart
abstracted the growing art
to a dissonant design
and a rich dream of paint,
on the grim basic plan
a varied white pigment

knifed and scrubbed, in one
corner a boiling brown
study in mahogany;
beige-biscuit left; right
a fat patch of white,
bread and milk in agony.

Rough brushwork here, thick
but vague; for already
behind these there loom
shades of the prehistoric,
ghosts of colour and form,
furniture, function, body –

as if to announce the death
of preconception and myth
and start again on the fresh
first morning of the world
with snow, ash, whitewash,
limestone, mother-of-pearl,

bleach, paper, soap, foam
and cold kitchen cream,
to find in the nitty-gritty
of surfaces and utensils
the shadow of a presence,
a long-sought community.

Roman Script

Nei rifiuti del mondo nasce un nuovo mondo.
– PASOLINI

I

Rain in the night; now cock-crow and engine-hum
wake us at first light on the Janiculum
and we open the shutters to extravagant mists
behind which an autumn sun hotly insists
on parasol pine, low dove and glistening drop,
bright lemon, jonquil, jasmine and heliotrope –
the Respighi moment, life mimicking art again
as when the fiddles provoke line-dancing rain.

II

Turn back into the room where sunlight shows
dim ceilings, domino tiles, baroque frescoes,
a scenic interior, a theatrical space
for Byronic masquerade or Goldoni farce,
vapours and swordsmanship, the cape and fan,
the amorous bad-boy and the glamorous nun,
boudoir philosophy, night music on balconies,
the gondola section nodding as in a sea breeze.

III

Rome of conspiracy theories and lost causes,
exiles have died here in your haunted palaces
where our own princes, flushed with wine and hope,
they say, and the squeal of a lone bagpipe
torn from the wild and windy western ocean,
dreamed up elaborate schemes of restoration –
a world more distant now than Pompeiian times
with the shipyards visible from the nymphaeums.

IV

Type up the new stuff, nap between four and five
when for a second time you come alive
with flies that linger in November light
and moths not even camphor puts to flight;
listen with them to sepia furniture
and piano practice from the flat next-door;
watch where the poplar spires of evening thin
to smoke-stains on the ochreous travertine.

V

Now out you go among the *botteghe oscure*
and fluttering street-lamps of Trastevere,
over the bridge where Fiat and Maserati
burn up the race-track of the eternal city,

floodlit naiad and triton; for at this hour
the beautiful and damned are in Harry's Bar
or setting out for pit-stops, sexy dives
and parties, as in the movie of our lives.

VI

Here they are, Nero, Julia, Diocletian
and the shrewd popes of a later dispensation
at ease in bath-house and in antiquarium
or raping young ones in the venial gym –
as the prophet said, as good a place as any
to watch the end of the world; to watch, at least,
the late mutation of the romantic egotist
when the knock comes at last for Don Giovanni.

VII

Snap out of your art fatigue and take a trip
to church and basilica, forum, fountain and frieze,
to the Sistine Chapel's violent comic-strip
or the soft marble thighs of Persephone; seize
real presence, the art-historical sublime,
in an intricate owl-blink Nikon moment of time,
in a flash-photography lightning storm above
Cecilia's actual body, Endymion's actual grave.

VIII

Mid-morning noise of prisoners playing hard
in the Regina Coeli's echoing exercise yard –
for even the wretched of the earth are here
with instructions to entertain the visitor;
and we walk in reality, framed as virtuality,
as in a film-set, Cinecittà, a cinema city
where life is a waking dream in broad daylight
and everything is scripted for our delight.

IX

Others were here, *comunque,* who dreamed in youth
of a society based on hope and truth –
the poet of internment, solitude, morning sea,
of the lost years when we used to fall in love
not with women themselves but some commodity,
a hat, a pair of shoes, a blouse, a glove
(to him death came with the eyes of a new age,
a glib post-war cynicism restyled as image).

X

and the poet of poverty, ash on the night wind,
starlight and tower blocks on waste ground,
peripheral rubbish dumps beyond the noise
of a circus, where sedated girls and boys

put out for a few bob on some building site
the cloudy imperium of ancient night
and in the ruins, amid disconsolate lives
on the edge of the artful city, a myth survives.

XI

His is the true direction we have lost
since his corpse showed up on the beach at Ostia
and life as we know it evolved into imagery,
production values, packaged history,
the genocidal corporate imperative
and the bright garbage on the incoming wave
best seen at morning rush-hour in driving rain:
"in the refuse of the world a new world is born".

XII

(*A Rewrite: Metastasio*)

I invent dreams and stories, and even as I outline
dreams and romances on the unwritten page
I enter into them with so soft a heart
I weep at evils of my own design.
I've more sense when not deceived by art;
the creative spirit is quiet then and rage,
love, genuine emotions, spring for once
from real life and from felt experience.

Ah, but words on the page aren't the whole story
for all my hopes and fears are fictions too
and I live in a virtual fever of creation —
the whole course of my life has been imagination,
my days a dream; when we wake from history
may we find peace in the substance of the true.

Medbh McGuckian

I felt these five illustrate some kind of development on my part. The first, "Waters", is a feminine one about feminine experience filtered through nature. Obviously the phrase "the waters breaking" has a strange fascination for a woman and a poet. It was an early poem that explored uncharted territory, acknowledging a woman's peculiar power and capacity to bear a child.

"Yeastlight" was an example of a love poem or an address to the Muse and the complications of living a private and public life honestly without compromising either, a problem we have just seen at its most horrific in the film about Cathal Ó Searchaigh. It is hard to be too careful in protecting the creative self from the suffering one.

"White Magpie" is an example of a historical political poem about Ireland, particularly its republican past, which I know so little about. This one was about the botched hanging of the Manchester Martyrs, where church and state seem equally cruel.

"Turning the Moon into a Verb" is about the difficulties facing the woman writer but also one of my many astronomical poems. I have a sister who loves the stars. "Viewing Neptune through a Telescope" is another of these. I like the way our planetary modernity throws us back on classic mythology in such a verbally productive way.

I hoped my choice might not depress people about the North's predicaments and could have selected many others that might have been narrower but these I felt were cheery on the whole.

Waters

In quiet streams, the buoyancy of water-lily leaves
Will take the even weight of a child on their celled floors;
The bamboo dies as soon as it has flowered, however scantily;
The sacred lotus opens wide on four successive nights.

A search round fern patches in the autumn will discern
A ribbon or a heart of simple moss that hugs the ground
Where spores have fallen – some have changed their leaves
To roots, and left the shore for the eternal spray of waterfalls.

Straw-coloured rhododendron trusses seem insensible
To snow, with their felted backs, of tan or silver brown:
The barrel-palm appreciates above its swollen trunk
The neat habits of camellias, the water-loss of dates.

Yeastlight

You speak like the rain, as if you were the weather.
I can almost see the passage of wine through your throat
As you swallow, its colour seems to be standing
Behind you, in the designer-blue air. When I found
In the very cup of the town those poems sewn
Into cushions, or pushed into saucepans or shoes,
I took the arm of someone I didn't know
Who turned over all my mattresses
And shook out every book.

I could not have imagined pearls had such warmth.
My house planned to catch the sun in all
Its rooms, in the shape of a fan, seemed no better
Than other houses; its clear note had gone out
And fallen in with the wind which sometimes
Sounds so much like rain, the passing
Of wise hands over shoulders, the frisking
Of clothing that remoulds you and restrains you,
Back into the narrow bed of a girl.

Still my dining-room, with its gold oak-leaf
Paper, has three long windows looking west
Upon a ligulate forest, and *famille rose,*
Famille verte, china for an up-with-the-kettle,

Round-with-the-car, man, if you could not bear
To have it going on one moment longer,
Doors with their fertile roar, their desert
Glances, closing from the inside, not the out
Or to have it ever stopped.

White Magpie

The black beams overhead,
they had been birch, pear and willow wood.
Remember well their blood-tunnel perfume
as it enters the refuge of your lips,
for a forest is a highly-perfumed dungeon,
hate-crested, gold-skinned,
a portable Tudor prison.

The prisoners, with washed faces,
were walking aft, one by one.
Will the slaver,
wearing the ring of her anchor,
be allowed to go to pieces where she lies,
moistening the blossomless sea-sand,
calmly waiting for the Angel Death?

Almost every head was uncovered
by a willingness to come out
and see a pageant pass;
a musk-duck swayed over
the off-horse Fleur-de-Lis
and stars, unknown before, kissed
his right cheek through the white cap.

My best river breathed an hour
after the dexterous stillness of the rope
and the smaller dark-pea thongs
down the wrists in front of the stomach
ceased beating the air.
Who will now buy the great ocean
avenue of his sodden necktie?

Turning the Moon into a Verb

A timeless winter
That wants to be now
Will go on taking shape in me.
Now everything can begin.

Everything can reach much
Further up; with this new
Listening, the longing at the window
For the missing season weakens.

When springtime had need of him,
He did not offer me the winter,
He took away each of the seasons
In its visual turn

Dark does that to you also,
And the headlessness
Of a turning of light that mentions a green
A little darker than all other greens.

A secret year, a secret time,
Its flight is a written image
Of its cry, its capacity for sound
I call spring, the experience

When the sky becomes a womb,
And a vision of rivers slanting
Across the doubly opened page
Of the moon turns her into a verb.

An image I have consciously
Broken like a shoulder on your hearing,
The inconstancy within constancy
That is the price of a month.

Viewing Neptune through a Glass Telescope

From my place on the coloured earth,
with my inner face of travel,
I could see nothing but the world as a whole,
our life of whirling steel

like a room composed in a quarrel
between covetousness and worship,
having an appetite for sounds
but no particular desires.

An aching fog walked through my flesh
from those homes created in space,
and the more streets I saw there
the less I had power to say

What else could one do but walk
those same streets in their grip of summer,
succumbing to summer's little freshness
as tree- or sea-birds sing the hours?

Grey, white and lavender,
volcanic and feathery,
the layers of memory that surface
as one moves into tomorrow

so lately embodied,
whose meanings are not meant for us,
fed upon the water
that placard of light in the air.

PAULA MEEHAN

Lest the other poems are eavesdropping let me say I chose these five poems not because I believe them better than the other poems but because after I finished them I felt I'd come across a threshold in the craft. They reconnected me to source and reminded me of the work's true nature.

The inspirations were as varied as Kit Smart, *Get Smart,* the Tarot, *The White Goddess,* Ms E. Bishop's "One Art", Hector McDonnell's painting of a figure in Bewley's Cafe, as well as events in my life as a citizen. A Masonite plant was being built on the banks of the Shannon during the writing of the earliest poem included here, "Well"; Shell Oil was injuncting local farmers and residents of Mayo, who ended up in Mountjoy Gaol for standing firm for the land, as "Death of a Field" was being written. That poem itself was impelled by Fingal County Council's dodgy development out the back of our house.

The "Mother" section of "On Poetry" came in a spurt when I read that metre and mother are of the same root in the Indo-European mother tongue. It came in about five minutes and I loved the tyranny of cycles, body and breath, that writing it broke for me. The villanelle "Quitting the Bars" took about five years from first note and stray lines to final version, which probably mirrors how long it took me to get used to sobriety.

I worked hard on these poems but they were ultimately given from outside myself, for which three deep bows of gratitude.

Well

I know this path by magic not by sight.
Behind me on the hillside the cottage light
is like a star that's gone astray. The moon
is waning fast, each blade of grass a rune
inscribed by hoarfrost. This path's well worn.
I lug a bucket by bramble and blossoming blackthorn.
I know this path by magic not by sight.
Next morning when I come home quite unkempt
I cannot tell what happened at the well.
You spurn my explanation of a sex spell
cast by the spirit who guards the source
that boils deep in the belly of the earth,
even when I show you what lies strewn
in my bucket – a golden waning moon,
seven silver stars, our own porch light,
your face at the window staring into the dark.

Home

I am the blind woman finding her way home by a map of
tune.
When the song that is in me is the song I hear from the
world
I'll be home. It's not written down and I don't remember
the words.
I know when I hear it I'll have made it myself. I'll be home.

A version I heard once in Leitrim was close, a wet Tuesday
night
in the Sean Relig bar. I had come for the session, I stayed
for the vision and lore. The landlord called time,
the music dried up, the grace notes were pitched to the dark.
When the jukebox blared out *I'd only four senses and he*
left me senseless,
I'd no choice but to take to the road. On Grafton Street in
November
I heard a mighty sound: a travelling man with a didgeridoo
blew me clear to Botany Bay. The tune too far back to
live in
but scribed on my bones. In a past life I may have
been Kangaroo,
rocked in my dreamtime, convict ships coming o'er the foam.

In the Puzzle Factory one winter I was sure I was home.
The talking in tongues, the riddles, the rhymes, struck a chord
that cut through the pharmaceutical haze. My rhythm catatonic,
I lulled myself back to the womb, my mother's heart
beating the drum of herself and her world. I was tricked
by her undersong, just close enough to my own. I took then
to dancing; I spun like a Dervish. I swear I heard the subtle
music of the spheres. It's no place to live, but –
out there in space, on your own, hung aloft the night.
The tune was in truth a mechanical drone;
I was a pitiful monkey jigging on cue. I came back to earth
with a land, to rain on my face, to sun in my hair. And
    grateful too.

The wisewomen say you must live in your skin, call *it* home,
no matter how battered or broken, misused by the world,
    you can heal.
This morning a letter arrived on the nine o'clock post.
The Department of Historical Reparation, and who did I
    blame?
The Nuns? Your Mother? The State? *Tick box provided,*
we'll consider your case. I'm burning my soapbox, I'm taking
the very next train. A citizen of nowhere, nothing to
    my name.

I'm on my last journey. Though my lines are all wonky
they spell me a map that makes sense. Where the song that
 is in me
is the song I hear from the world, I'll set down my burdens
and sleep. The spot that I lie on at last the place I'll call
 home.

On Poetry

for Niamh Morris

VIRGIN

       To look back then:
       one particular moon snared in the willows
       and there I am sleeping in my body,
       a notebook beside me with girl poems in it
       and many blank pages to fill
       and let there be a rose and the memory of its thorn
       and a scar on my thigh where the thorn had ripped

       earlier that day in the abandoned garden
       where he came first to me
       and lifted my skirt
       and we sank to the ground

       And let me be peaceful
       for I wasn't.
       Not then, nor for many moons after.

MOTHER

       mother you terrorist
       muck mother mud mother
       you chewed me up
       you spat me out

mother you devourer
plucker of my soul bird
mammal self abuser
nightmatrix huntress

mother keeper
of calendar and keys
ticking off moon days
locking up the grain

mother house and tomb
your two breasts storing
strontium and lies when
you created time

mother you created plenty
you and your serpent consort
you and your nests
you and your alphabets

mother your pictographs
your mandalas your runes
your inches your seconds
your logic your grammar

mother wearing a necklace of skulls
who calls into being
by uttering the name
mater logos metric

mother your skirts
your skins your pelts
with your charms
old cow I'm your calf

mother fetishist
heart breaker
forsaker and fool
in the pouring rain

mother I stand
over your grave
and your granite headstone
and I weep

WHORE

I Iearnt it well. l learnt it early on:
that nothing's free, that everything is priced
and easier do the business, be cute, be wized
up and sussed, commodify the fun

than barter flesh in incremental spite
the way the goodwives/girlfriends did
pretending to be meek and do as bid
while close-managing their menfolk. It wasn't right.

I believed it wasn't right. See me now −
I'm old and blind and past my sexual prime
and it's been such a long and lonely time
since I felt fire in my belly. I must allow

there'll be no chance of kindling from my trance
the spark that wakes the body into dance;
yet still comes unbidden like god's gift: an image −
a boy turns beneath me, consolatory and strange.

Death of a Field

The field itself is lost the morning it becomes a site
When the Notice goes up: Fingal County Council – 44 houses

The memory of the field is lost with the loss of its herbs

Though the woodpigeons in the willow
And the finches in what's left of the hawthorn hedge
And the wagtail in the elder
Sing on their hungry summer song

The magpies sound like flying castanets

And the memory of the field disappears with its flora:
Who can know the yearning of yarrow
Or the plight of the scarlet pimpernel
Whose true colour is orange?

And the end of the field is the end of the hidey holes
Where first smokes, first tokes, first gropes
Were had to the scentless mayweed

The end of the field as we know it is the start of the estate
The site to be planted with houses each two or three
        bedroom
Nest of sorrow and chemical, cargo of joy

The end of dandelion is the start of Flash
The end of dock is the start of Pledge
The end of teazel is the start of Ariel
The end of primrose is the start of Brillo
The end of thistle is the start of Bounce
The end of sloe is the start of Oxyaction
The end of herb robert is the start of Brasso
The end of eyebright is the start of Fairy

Who amongst us is able to number the end of grasses
To number the losses of each seeding head?

                     I'll walk out once
Barefoot under the moon to know the field
Through the soles of my feet to hear
The myriad leaf lives green and singing
The million million cycles of being in wing

That — before the field become solely map memory
In some archive of some architect's screen
I might possess it or it possess me
Through its night dew, its moon white caul
Its slick and shine and its profligacy
In every wingbeat in every beat of time

Quitting the Bars

Quitting's hard but staying sober's harder.
The day by day; the drudge and boredom bit;
not sure if the self is cell or warder.

You quit the bars; you quit the sordid ardour;
you quit the tulpas sucking on your tit.
Quitting's hard but staying sober's harder.

You sometimes think you got away with murder.
The shady souls regard you as you sit –
you wonder if they are wards or warders

in this sad café. The mind's last border
dissolves. Guilt has done a midnight flit.
Quitting's hard but staying sober's harder.

So sip cool water; the light's a wonder
streaming out in wave-particles. You've lit
up bright your prison cell. Body – warder

of your dreams – will be the dreams' recorder,
though wrapped now in a skin that doesn't fit.
Quitting's hard but staying sober's harder;
stranger for your being both ward and warder.

JOHN MONTAGUE

Of course I would be glad to play on the Poolbeg Gaelic Rules team, and will not inquire as to who the other players are. I would put Kennelly in goal, however, and Hartnett at full forward. Very nippy! As to the five poems, I am growing weary of my own golden oldies, those poems that I read to audiences and which are often requested by them. And now there is the Leaving Cert, with "The Cage" and "The Locket" breaking young hearts in the Republic.

I find that, ironically, public readings can nearly misrepresent a writer's body of work. He or she will choose to read funny poems or dramatic ones, but not necessarily those that best express or embody the author's deepest feelings. And for me there is the additional impediment of a stammer, which has often prevented me from reading those poems I cherish most, because they are so charged with feeling that I might falter over them.

So I suggest "Courtyard in Winter", which was written about a North American friend who committed suicide in London not too long after Sylvia Plath. And "A Flowering Absence", which goes to the heart of my own early trauma and mystery. Also "Herbert Street Revisited", which is a homage to a broken marriage. These are in my *Collected Poems,* and there is a strong poem for my dead brother in my newest collection, *Drunken Sailor,* called "Last Court".

These would make for a fine statement, as far as I am concerned. It might seem a little melancholy, so I would also suggest one of the meditations, like "Mount Eagle" (from the book of that name, and also in the *Collected Poems*).

Courtyard in Winter

Snow curls in on the cold wind.

Slowly, I push back the door.
After long absence, old habits
Are painfully revived, those disciplines
Which enable us to survive,
To keep a minimal fury alive
While flake by faltering flake

Snow curls in on the cold wind.

Along the courtyard, the boss
Of each cobblestone is rimmed
In white, with winter's weight
Pressing, like a silver shield,
On all the small plots of earth,
Inert in their living death as

Snow curls in on the cold wind.

Seized in a giant fist of frost,
The grounded planes at London Airport,
Mallarmé swans, trapped in ice.
The friend whom I have just left
Will be dead, a year from now,
Through her own fault, while

Snow curls in on the cold wind.

Or smothered by some glacial truth?
Thirty years ago, I learnt to reach
Across the rusting hoops of steel
That bound our greening waterbarrel
To save the living water beneath
The hardening crust of ice, before

Snow curls in on the cold wind.

But despair has a deeper crust.
In all our hours together, I never
Managed to ease the single hurt
That edged her towards her death;
Never reached through her loneliness
To save a trust, chilled after

Snow curls in on the cold wind.

I plunged through snowdrifts once,
Above our home, to carry
A telegram to a mountain farm.
Fearful but inviting, they waved me
To warm myself at the flaring
Hearth before I faced again where

Snow curls in on the cold wind.

The news I brought was sadness.
In a far city, someone of their name
Lay dying. The tracks of foxes,
Wild birds, as I climbed down
Seemed to form a secret writing
Minute and frail as life when

Snow curls in on the cold wind.

Sometimes, I know that message.
There is a disease called snow-sickness;
The glare from the bright god,
The earth's reply. As if that
Ceaseless, glittering light was
All the truth we'd left after

Snow curls in on the cold wind.

So, before dawn, comfort fails.
I imagine her end, in some sad
Bedsitting room, the steady hiss
Of the gas more welcome than an
Act of friendship, the protective
Oblivion of a lover's caress if

Snow curls in on the cold wind.

In the canyon of the street
The dark snowclouds hesitate,
Turning to slush almost before
They cross the taut canvas of
The street stalls, the bustle
Of a sweeper's brush after

Snow curls in on the cold wind.

The walls are spectral, white.
All the trees black-ribbed, bare.
Only veins of ivy, the sturdy
Laurel with its waxen leaves,
Its scant red berries, survive
To form a winter wreath as

Snow curls in on the cold wind.

What solace but endurance, kindness?
Against her choice, I still affirm
That nothing dies, that even from
Such bitter failure memory grows;
The snowflake's structure, fragile
But intricate as the rose when

Snow curls in on the cold wind.

A Flowering Absence

How can one make an absence flower,
lure a desert to sudden bloom?
Taut with terror, I rehearse a time
when I was taken from a sick room
as before from your flayed womb.

And given away to be fostered
wherever charity could afford.
I came back, lichened with sores,
from the care of still poorer
immigrants, new washed from the hold.

I bless their unrecorded names,
whose need was greater than mine,
wet nurses from tenement darkness
giving suck for a time,
because their milk was plentiful

Or their own children gone.
They were the first to succour
that still terrible thirst of mine,
a thirst for love and knowledge,
to learn something of that time

Of confusion, poverty, absence.
Year by year, I track it down
intent for a hint of evidence,
seeking to manage the pain –
how a mother gave away her son.

I took the subway to the hospital
in darkest Brooklyn, to call
on the old nun who nursed you
through the travail of my birth
to come on another cold trail.

"Sister Virgilius, how strange!
She died, just before you came.
She was delirious, rambling of all
her old patients; she could well
have remembered your mother's name".

Around the bulk of St Catherine's
another wild, raunchier Brooklyn:
as tough a territory as I've known,
strutting young Puerto Rican hoods,
flash of blade, of bicycle chain.

Mother, my birth was the death
of your love life, the last man
to flutter near your tender womb:
a neonlit bar sign winks off & on,
motherfucka, thass your name.

There is an absence, real as presence.
In the mornings I hear my daughter
chuckle, with runs of sudden joy.
Hurt, she rushes to her mother,
as I never could, a puling boy.

All roads wind backwards to it.
An unwanted child, a primal hurt.
I caught fever on the big boat
that brought us away from America –
away from my lost parents.

Surely my father loved me,
teaching me to croon, *Ragtime Cowboy
Joe, swaying in his saddle
as he sings,* as he did, drunkenly
dropping in from the speakeasy.

So I found myself shipped back
to his home, in an older country,
transported to a previous century,
where his sisters restored me,
natural love flowering around me.

And the hurt ran briefly underground
to break out in a schoolroom
where I was taunted by a mistress
who hunted me publicly down
to near speechlessness.

"So this is our brightest infant?
Where did he get that outlandish accent?
What do you expect, with no parents,
sent back from some American slum:
none of you are to speak like him!"

Stammer, impediment, stutter:
she had found my lode of shame,
and soon I could no longer utter
those magical words I had begun
to love, to dolphin delight in.

And not for two stumbling decades
would I manage to speak straight again.
Grounded for the second time
my tongue became a rusted hinge
until the sweet oils of poetry

eased it and grace flooded in.

Herbert Street Revisited
for Madeleine

I

A light is burning late
in this Georgian Dublin street:
someone is leading our old lives!

And our black cat scampers again
through the wet grass of the convent garden
upon his masculine errands.

The pubs shut: a released bull,
Behan shoulders up the street,
topples into our basement, roaring "John!"

A pony and donkey cropped
flank by flank under the trees opposite;
short neck up, long neck down,

as Nurse Mullen knelt by her bedside
to pray for her lost Mayo hills,
the bruised bodies of Easter Volunteers.

Animals, neighbours, treading the pattern
of one time and place into history,
like our early marriage, while

tall windows looked down upon us
from walls flushed light pink or salmon
watching and enduring succession.

II

As I leave, you whisper,
"Don't betray our truth,"
and like a ghost dancer,
invoking a lost tribal strength,
I halt in tree-fed darkness
to summon back our past,
and celebrate a love that eased
so kindly, the dying bone,
enabling the spirit to sing
of old happiness, when alone.

III

So put the leaves back on the tree,
put the tree back in the ground,
let Brendan trundle his corpse down
the street singing, like Molly Malone.

Let the black cat, tiny emissary
of our happiness, streak again
through the darkness, to fall soft
clawed into a landlord's dustbin.

Let Nurse Mullen take the last
train to Westport, and die upright
in her chair, facing a window
warm with the blue slopes of Nephin.

And let the pony and donkey come –
look, someone has left the gate open –
like hobbyhorses linked in
the slow motion of a dream
parading side by side, down
the length of Herbert Street,
rising and falling, lifting
their hooves through the moonlight.

Last Court

Poetry, 'tis a court of judgement upon the soul.
– HENRIK IBSEN

1

Non piangere

From your last chair,
two months before that glutton, cancer,
devoured you, lawyer brother,
you gave me a final wigging, read the riot act,
as if I were some juvenile delinquent
hauled before the magistrate.

This sun-warm conservatory,
latest addition to your ultra-modern bungalow
overlooking Brown-Lecky's estate,
(now manicured golf course) recalls the deck
of that Cunard liner, the *Cameronia,*
which, ages ago, shipped us boys to Fintona.

Home again, in mid-Tyrone,
you built your now fading life,
fathering a tribe within a tribe,
only to chide me now, for my "great mistake,
repeated, *twice*", of choosing a wife
from the wider world outside.

"They don't understand. You need somebody who
thinks like you, shares your beliefs."
Mildly, I place a picture of your two nieces
(my Cork, French, Jewish,
Church of Ireland children)
upon your knee, for loving avuncular scrutiny

But you sigh it away
and, having pronounced your last verdict,
stalk off to rest, dying, but striding with dignity,
without a whimper of self-pity,
through your assembled family,
your last gift, this fragile bravery.

2

To leave me forever, with your disapproval,
yet rueful love, and a contradictory testimony,
"Strangely, I have never felt so happy, as now,
giving up, letting go, floating free."
You look down, pensively, at your glass
of burnished Black Bush whiskey.

"And, no, I no longer pray,
although I talk to God sometimes in my head.
And our parents. Why did you hurt our mother's pride
with your mournful auld poem, *The Dead Kingdom*?
Only a child, you couldn't understand their decision:
besides, you got the details wrong!"

"So you believe we'll see them again?
Bone-light, transfigured, Molly and Jim
angels dancing upon a pin, and then
I can take it up with them again?"
"No," you say stubbornly, "never again,"
shaking your once-red Ulster head.

And plucking your pallid, freckled arm,
"I don't believe," you proclaim,
"in the body's resurrection.
See how the flesh wastes parchment-thin?"
Yet, resigned as the Dying Gaul,
stoic as an ancient Roman.

3

Un grido lacerante

Dear freckled brother, in an old photo,
you throw your arm around me
in a Brooklyn park, your impulse to hug
preserved there for posterity.
Let me reverse our roles, carefully as I can,
to encircle you, this time, with *my* arm.

In far off Florence, I learnt of your death;
Evelyn calling from a rain-swept West Cork.
"It was a merciful release," that cliché – yet true.
"But how can I trek all that way North?
My sister's children are here, as well as our own.
It's a long hard slog up to County Tyrone."

Phone to my ear, gazing out at the Arno,
I hear, behind her, the laughter of children,
those nieces whose picture you dismissed.
"Cherish the living, while honouring the dead,
I'll stand over that, pray they'll comprehend.
The church bells of Florence will bless him instead."

As many mourners assemble at your funeral
in our chill and distant Northern chapel
since you loved paintings I patrol
the Pitti, the Uffizi, turning from
a foam-borne Botticelli nymph, or
grave Madonna, to weep above Dante's city:

sharp-tempered, once you smashed me to the floor in
our mother's kitchen, and standing over
me, like some American boxer, "Rise
and fight like a man" – and I only sixteen!
Aproned Molly hovering, a hapless referee;
you stalk away, to return with a brusque apology.

Sharp-tempered but kindly, you drove
your poet brother home from Dublin,
emptying my squalid flat without reproach.
Later, wives and lives came between us,
differing codes of conduct and belief.
Yet I still glimpse your ginger hair and freckle face.

Long before the cancer struck, I saw that face
grown ashen, fissured as chalk, suddenly old
as though some secret source had parched,
and sought to tell you, *Relax again,*
as when you roamed Bundoran with the Fintona gang.
But tact forbade. Or cowardice?

Now, hear my plea. Sweet-souled Santayana
might have agreed with you, brother, about exogamy,
but against your patriarchal views,
I assert the right of love to choose,
from whatever race, or place. And of verse
to allay, to heal, our tribal curse, that narrowness.

Mount Eagle

1

The eagle looked at this changing world;
Sighed and disappeared into the mountain.

Before he left he had a last reconnoitre:
the multi-coloured boats in the harbour

nodded their masts and a sandy white
crescent of strand smiled back at him.

How he liked the slight, drunk lurch
of the fishing fleet, the tide hoist-

ing them a little, at their ropes' end.
Beyond, wrack, and the jutting rocks

emerging, slowly, monsters stained
and slimed with strands of seaweed.

Ashore, beached boats and lobsterpots,
settled as hens in the sand.

2

Content was life in its easiest form;
Another was the sudden growling storm

which the brooding eagle preferred,
bending his huge wings into the winds'

wild buffeting, or thrusting down along
the wide sky, at an angle, slideways

to survey the boats, scurrying homewards,
tacking against the now contrary winds,

all of whom he knew by their names.
To be angry in the morning, calmed

by midday, but brooding again in
the evening was all in a day's quirk

with lengthy intervals for silence,
gliding along, like a blessing, while

the fleet toiled on earnestly beneath
him, bulging with a fine day's catch.

3

But now he had to enter the mountain.
Why? Because a cliff had asked him?

The whole world was changing, with one
language dying; and another encroaching,

bright with buckets, cries of children.
There seemed to be no end to them,

and the region needed a guardian –
so the mountain had told him. And

a different destiny lay before him:
to be the spirit of that mountain.

Everyone would stand in awe of him.
When he was wrapped in the mist's caul

they would withdraw because of him,
peer from behind blind or curtain.

When he lifted his wide forehead
bold with light, in the morning,

they would all laugh and smile with him.
It was a greater task than an eagle's

aloofness, but sometimes, under his oilskin
of coiled mist, he sighs for lost freedom.

SINÉAD MORRISSEY

I've chosen five, as yet uncollected, poems which sit in a sequence to do with pregnancy and birth. "Storm" was written in a writers' centre in Switzerland. I liken the little girl in the photographs on the wall, who I had assumed was the patroness of the chateau as a child, to Alice. Two days after writing the poem, I discovered that the little girl was Alice – that the photographs were Lewis Carroll originals. This sequence begins and ends with faces at the window – with another world pressing against this one, and its focus is the connection between birth and death, and the way in which both birth and death punch a hole through to an elsewhere we cannot hope to understand.

Storm

It was already Gothic
enough, what with that
King-of-Versailles-size bed
with room for me and two
or three liveried footmen;

wall-lights like candle-shafts
in fake pearl and cut
glass; and the stranded
little girl in the photographs
growing sorrowful –

her cascade sleeves, her floral
crown – as though taken
by Lewis Carroll. All afternoon
the church bells rang out
their warning. Cumulostratus

ascended into heaven.
Evening and the white forked
parting of the sky fell
directly overhead, casements
rattled on hinges and Thunder

may as well have summoned
the raggle-taggle denizens
of his vociferous world:
the ghouls, the gashed, the dead
so bored by now of being

dead they flock to gawk –
sanctuary was still sanctuary
except more so, with the inside
holding flickeringly, and the
outside clamouring in.

Apocrypha

When I was ten and convinced
I would never have children

simply by keeping my underwear on
at night-time, I was disarmed

by the history
of Mary Ann Sexton —

mother, camp-follower, picker
of pockets, stower of teeth —

and of how her womb
was pierced by a bullet

still wet from the testicle
of a Roundhead Lieutenant

at the Battle of Marston Moor.
As though the slaughter itself

required climax and sought out
the unlikeliest agents, or

a new king pined
to be born, this was as improbable

a conception
as the physical laws of the earth

and all the revolving planets
could allow.

What hope was underwear now?
If destiny hovered

with green wings and a stained,
indefatigable purpose

over my bedspread,
I, too, would be done for.

Found Architecture
for Kerry Hardie

These days are all about waiting. What would you say
if I tried to explain how my single true activity
this wet and shivery May is "found architecture"?

As the giver of an Italian kaleidoscope
that makes its heel–toe shapes, not from beads or seeds
or painted meticulous details, but from the room,

from whatever room I happen to be in,
or from the street, always eager and unerringly
democratic, you stand slightly to the south of me

with your head raised and I imagine you smiling.
The day it arrived I mangled the blue of the bathroom
with the pistachio green of my bedroom ceiling

and sat entranced: such symmetrical splicing
of everything, anything, to make of my waiting-house
a star-pointed frame that entered and left

itself behind as the cylinder turned. Any light that there was
was instantly mystical – a crack in the pattern's
typography, like the door at the end of the corridor

shedding radiance. Yesterday evening, by the sea,
a strangled sealed-off swamp by a walkway
threw up, suddenly, the Aboriginal outback:

rotted glands of a pond between knee-high grasses
and a white tree undoing itself in its ink-stained
surfaces. The tree looked like a crocodile's ribcage

as I passed along the perimeter, or the wide-propped
jawbone of a whale. Until it became, the further
I walked, a canoe, asleep on the water and fettered

with algae. Another dead branch sat up
in the grass like the head of an otter and talked.
This, too, was found architecture. And all the usual,

of course: skeletons of geranium leaves on windowsills
long afterwards; snake skins, clouds.
Beaches are full of it: found architecture being

the very business of beaches. Most recently
(and most disarmingly) this: handed to me in a roll
of four like mug-shot photographs from a machine,

his seahorse spine, his open-shut anemone
of a heart, and the row of unbelievable teeth
shining high in the crook of his skull as though back-

stitched into place. From blood and the body's
inconsolable hunger I have been my own kaleidoscope –
five winter-bleached girls on a diving board, ready to jump.

"Love, the Nightwatch ..."

Love, the nightwatch, gloved and gowned, attended.
Your father held my hand. His hands grew bruised
and for days afterwards wore a green and purple
    coverlet

when he held you to the light, held your delicate,
    dented
head, thumbed-in like a water font. They used
stopwatches, clipcharts, the distant hoofbeats of a
    heart

(divined, it seemed, by radio, so your call fell
    interwined
with taxicabs, police reports, the weather blowing
    showery
from the north) and a beautiful fine white cane,

carved into a fish hook. I was a haystack the children
    climbed
and ruined, collapsing almost imperceptibly
at first, then caving in spectacularly as you stuttered
    and came

– crook-shouldered, blue, believable, beyond me –
in a thunder of blood, in a flood-plain of intimate
    stains.

Through the Square Window

In my dream the dead have arrived
to wash the windows of my house.
There are no blinds to shut them out with.

The clouds above the Lough are stacked
like the clouds are stacked above Delft.
They have the glutted look of clouds over water.

The heads of the dead are huge. I wonder
if it's my son they're after, his
effortless breath, his ribbon of years –

but he sleeps on unregarded in his cot,
inured, it would seem, quite naturally
to the sluicing and battering and paring back of glass

that delivers this shining exterior . . .
One blue boy holds a rag in his teeth
between panes like a conjuror.

And then, as suddenly as they came, they go.
And there is a horizon
from which only the clouds stare in,

the massed canopies of Hazelbank,
the severed tip of the Strangford Peninsula,
and a density in the room I find it difficult to breathe in

until I wake, flat on my back with a cork
in my mouth, stopper-bottled, in fact,
like a herbalist's cure for dropsy.

Nuala Ní Dhomhnaill

The five best poems that would represent my work, from where I stand at present, are as follows.

"Leaba Shíoda": The reason I chose this poem is because it was the first time I felt I had euphonically mastered the Feminine Principle. Until then I was a bit of a space cadet, living entirely in the mind. This was the first time I wrote the "language of the body". It was very important for me developmentally, both psychologically and artistically.

"Máthair": One way or another my mother has been my most important muse. Because of unfortunate incidents of illness and absence in my early childhood and then Alzheimer's in her old age, we never really got to understand each other. Note, though, that this poem is called "Máthair" not "mo mháthair". I wrote it in Turkey, from which angle of difference the particular Irish phenomenon of the "Irish Mammy", a very capable woman who, because of the marriage ban, could not work, but rather experienced life vicariously through her children, coupled with a mostly absent father, whose basic involvement in family life was just to bring home the bacon, seemed to me a particularly Irish form of dysfunction.

The third poem I would have to choose would be "An Crann", translated in *Pharaoh's Daughter* by Paul Muldoon as "As for the Quince". This is where I suddenly discovered that the béaloideas stories that I had grown up with and that were are all around me were not just some twee antiquated fantasies but could be used by a writer in a completely different matter for sociological and psychological enquiry, in the most modern or even post-modern way. This was a mind-blowing revelation, thanks to the folklore collector Joe Daly, whom I knew well in West Kerry and who advised me when I felt lonely in Dublin to go into the Irish Folklore Archives in UCD. "Feic a bhfeicfir", were the words he used to me, which might be best translated as "to see what you might see". And I surely saw a lot, and fell into a goldmine, the mining of which will keep me out of mischief until the end of my days. Once again the poem is about intrusion or interference, and that is why Paul Muldoon's slight changes are perfectly in keeping with it, because otherwise, how do you intrude English into English in the sinister way that it intrudes on the Irish text in the original?

The next poem must surely be a love poem, as I have written all too many of these. Among many possibilities, I choose "An Bhean Mhídhílis", which I got at first from the wonderful Máire Mhac an tSaoi translation of Lorca's original. Later, reading the original in Spanish with a dual-language text, it dawned on me that Lorca, though brilliant, had not perhaps got the woman's side of the story quite right, so I set out to rectify that situation. The fact that it is in a stripped-down version of a traditional metre, "meadracht an amhráin", adds to the joke, as nobody was expecting such a modern "get-off-your-kit" poem in a traditional metre.

The last poem has to be "Dubh", a poem so unlike anything I have written before or since that I still wonder at the aesthetic behind it. All I know is that I was in a mad rage at us so-called Europeans who allowed Ratko Mladic into the so-called "safe area" of Srebrenica. My mother-in-law had been a full-blood Bosnian Muslim from Sarajevo, though born and bred in Turkey after the Exchange of Populations. Any of those young men being separated onto those buses and driven to their doom could have been my son: the long thin bones, the once blonde hair gone dark with the appearance of testosterone, the navy blue eyes and Slavic cheekbones. What made me even madder was a meal I had gone to the previous Thursday, just before the news blackout, with some luminary Irish academics, only to find that they had no interest at all in Bosnia, because Catholic Northerners were not, for once, the victims. The poem is not about the people of Bosnia; for them I dare not speak. The poem is about my own attempt to structure in some way the dreadful self-anger I felt and to try, by wresting the language beyond its capabilities, maybe, to speak the unspeakable. The repetition of "Dubh, Dubh Dubh" is of course the sound of the gunshots killing the people, though that didn't dawn on me until a few weeks after I had written it.

An Crann

Do tháinig bean an leasa
le *Black and Decker*,
do ghearr sí anuas mo chrann.
D'fhanas im óinseach ag féachaint uirthi
faid a bhearraigh sí na brainsí
ceann ar cheann.

Tháinig m'fhear céile abhaile tráthnóna.
Chonaic sé an crann.
Bhí an gomh dearg air,
ní nach ionadh. Dúirt sé
"Canathaobh nár stopais í?
Nó cad is dóigh léi?
Cad a cheapfadh sí
dá bhfaighinnse *Black and Decker*
is dul chun a tí
agus crann ansúd a bhaineas léi,
a ghearradh anuas sa ghairdín?"

Tháinig bean ar leasa thar n-ais ar maidin.
Bhíos fós ag ithe mo bhricfeasta.
D'iarr sí orm cad dúirt m'fhear céile.
Dúrtsa léi cad dúirt sé,

As for the Quince
(translated by Paul Muldoon)

There came this bright young thing
with a Black and Decker
and cut down my quince-tree.
I stood with my mouth hanging open
while one by one
she trimmed off the branches.

When my husband got home that evening
and saw what had happened
he lost the rag,
as you can imagine.
"Why didn't you stop her?
What would she think
if I took the Black and Decker
round to her place
and cut down a quince-tree
belonging to her?
What would she make of that?"

Her ladyship came next morning
while I was at breakfast.
She enquired about his reaction.
I told her straight

go ndúirt sé cad is dóigh léi,
is cad a cheapfadh sí
dá bhfaigheadh sé siúd *Black and Decker*
is dul chun a tí
is crann ansúd a bhaineas léi
a ghearradh anuas sa ghairdín.

"Ó," ar sise, "*That's very interesting.*"
Bhí béim ar an *very*.
Bhí cling leis an *—ing*.
Do labhair sí ana-chiúin.
Bhuel, b'shin mo lá-sá,
pé ar bith sa tsaol é,
ionaithe bunoscionn.
Thit an tóin as mo bholg
is faoi mar a gheobhainn lascadh cic
nó leacadar sna baotháin
lion taom anbhainne isteach orm
a dhein chomh lag sam mé
gurb ar éigin a bhí ardú na méire ionam
as san go ceann trí lá.

Murab ionann is an crann
a dh'fhan ann, slán.

that he was wondering how she'd feel
if he took a Black and Decker
round to her house
and cut down a quince-tree of hers,
et cetera et cetera.

"O," says she, "that's very interesting."
There was a stress on the "very".
She lingered over the "ing".
She was remarkably calm and collected.
These are the times that are in it, so
All a bit topsy-turvy.
The bottom falling out of my belly
as if I had got a kick up the arse
or a punch in the kidneys.
A fainting-fit coming over me
that took the legs from under me
and left me so zonked
I could barely lift a finger
till Wednesday.

As for the quince, it was safe and sound
and still somehow holding its ground.

Máthair

Do thugais dom gúna
is thógais arís é;
do thugais dom capall
a dhíolais i m'éagmais;
do thugais dom cláirseach
is d'iarrais thar n-ais é;
do thugais dom beatha.

Féile Uí Bhrain
is a dhá shúil ina dhiaidh.

Cad déarfá?
dá stracfainn an gúna?
dá mbáfainn an capall?
dá scriosfainn an chláirseach
ag tachtadh sreanga an aoibhnis
is sreanga na beatha?
dá shiúlfainn le haill
thar imeall Cuas Cromtha?
ach tá's agam do fhreagra, –
le d'aigne mheánaoiseach
d'fhógrófá marbh mé,
is ar cháipéisí leighis
do scríobhfaí na focail
mí-bhuíoch, scitsifréineach.

Mother

You gave me a dress
and then took it back from me.
You gave me a horse
which you sold in my absence.
You gave me a harp
and then you asked me back for it.
And you gave me life.

At the miser's dinner-party
every bite is counted.

What would you say
if I tore the dress
if I drowned the horse
if I broke the harp
if I choked the strings
the strings of life?
Even if
I walked off a cliff?
I know your answer.

With your medieval mind
you'd announce me dead
and on the medical reports
you'd write the words
"ingrate, schizophrenic".

An Bhean Mhídhílis

Do phioc sé suas mé
ag an gcúntúirt
is tar éis beagáinín cainte
do thairg deoch dom
nár eitíos uaidh
is do shuíomair síos
ag comhrá.
Chuamair ó dheoch go deoch
is ó *joke* go *joke*
is do bhíos ólta
ní dúrt leis go rabhas pósta.

Dúirt sé go raibh carr aige
is ar theastaigh síob abhaile uaim
is ní fada ar an mbóthair
nó gur bhuail an teidhe é.
Do tharraing sé isteach ag *lay-by*
chun gurbh fhusaide mé a phógadh.
Bhí málaí plaisteacha ar na seacha
is bruscar ag gabháil lastuas dóibh
is nuair a leag sé a lámh idir mo cheathrúna
ní dúrt leis go rabhas pósta.

The Unfaithful Wife
(translated by Paul Muldoon)

He started coming on to me
at the spirit-grocer's warped and wonky counter
and after a preliminary spot of banter
offered to buy me a glass of porter;
I wasn't one to demur
and in no time at all we were talking
the hind leg off a donkey.
A quick succession of snorts and snifters
and his relentless repartee
had me splitting my sides with laughter.
However much the drink had loosened my tongue
I never let on I was married.

He would ask me if he could leave me home
in his famous motoring-car,
though we hadn't gone very far down that road
when he was overtaken by desire.
He pulled into a lay-by
the better to heap me with kisses.
There were plastic bags bursting with rubbish
stacked against the bushes.
Even as he slipped his hand between my thighs
I never let on I was married.

Bhí sé cleachtaithe deaslámhach
ag oscailt chnaipí íochtair mo ghúna,
ag lapadáil go barr mo stocaí
is an cneas bog os a gcionnsan
is nuair a bhraith sé
nach raibh bríste orm
nach air a tháinig giúmar
as cé thógfadh orm ag an nóiméad sin
ná dúrt leis go rabhas pósta.

He was so handy,
too, when it came to unbuttoning my dress
and working his way past my stocking-tops
to the soft skin just above.
When it dawns on him
that I wasn't wearing panties
things were definitely on the up and up
and it hardly seemed the appropriate moment
to let on I was married.

Leaba Shíoda

Do chóireoinn leaba duit
i Leaba Shíoda
sa bhféar ard
faoi iomrascáil na gcrann
is bheadh do chraiceann ann
mar shíoda ar shíoda
sa doircheacht
am lonnaithe na leamhan.

Craiceann a shníonn
go gléineach thar do ghéaga
mar bhainne á dháil as crúiscíní
am lóin
is tréad gabhar ag gabháil thar chnocáin
do chuid gruaige
cnocáin ar a bhfuil faillte arda
is dhá ghleann atá domhain.

Is bheadh do bheola taise
ar mhilseacht shiúcra
tráthnóna is sinn ag spaisteoireacht
cois abhann
is na gaotha meala
ag séideadh thar an Sionna
is na fiúisí ag beannú duit
ceann ar cheann.

Labysheedy (The Silken Bed)
(translated by Nuala Ní Dhomhnaill)

I'd make a bed for you
in Labysheedy
in the tall grass
under the wrestling trees
where your skin
would be silk upon silk
in the darkness
when the moths are coming down.

Skin which glistens
shining over your limbs
like milk being poured
from jugs at dinnertime;
your hair is a herd of goats
moving over rolling hills,
hills that have high cliffs
and two ravines.

And your damp lips
would be as sweet as sugar
at evening and we walking
by the riverside
with honeyed breezes
blowing over the Shannon
and the fuchsias bowing down to you
one by one.

Na fiúisí ag ísliú
a gceanna maorga
ag umhlú síos don áilleacht
os a gcomhair
is do phriocfainn péire acu
mar shiogairlíní
is do mhaiseoinn do chluasa
mar bhrídeog.

Ó, chóireoinn leaba duit
i Leaba Shíoda
le hamhascarnach an lae
i ndeireadh thall
is ba mhór an pléisiúr dúinn
bheith géaga ar ghéaga
ag iomrascáil
am lonnaithe na leamhan.

The fuchsias bending low
their solemn heads in obeisance to the beauty
in front of them
I would pick a pair of flowers
as pendant earrings
to adorn you
like a bride in shining clothes.

O I'd make a bed for you
in Labysheedy,
in the twilight hour
with evening falling slow
and what a pleasure it would be
to have our limbs entwine
wrestling
while the moths are coming down.

Dubh

ar thitim Shrebrenice, 11ú Iúil 1995

Is lá dubh é seo.
Tá an spéir dubh.
Tá an fharraige dubh.
Tá na gairdíní dubh.

Tá na crainn dubh.
Tá na cnoic dubh.
Tá na busanna dubh.
Tá na carranna a thugann na páistí ar scoil ar maidin dubh.

Tá na siopaí dubh.
Tá na bhfuinneoga dubh.
Tá na sráideanna dubh (is ní le daoine é).
Tá na nuachtáin a dhíolann an cailín dubh go bhfuil an
    folt láidir dubh uirthi
dubh dubh dubh.

Tá an damh dubh.
Tá an gadhar dubh.
Tá capall úd Uíbh Ráthaigh dubh.
Tá gach corréan a scinneann amach as an ealta dubh.
An chaora dhubh a sheasann amach de ghnáth i lár an tréada,
ní heisceacht í níos mó mar tá na caoirigh ar fad dubh.

242

Black

On the fall of Srebrenica, 11 July 1995
(translated by Paul Muldoon)

A black day, this.
The sky is black.
The sea is black.

The gardens are black.
The trees are black.
The hills are black.
The buses are black.
The cars bringing the kids to school are black.

The shops are black.
Their windows are black.
The streets are black (and I don't mean with people).
The newspapers sold by the dark girl with the great head of
  dark hair
Are black, black, black.

The ox is black.
The hound is black.
The very horse from Iveragh is black.
The bird suddenly out of sync with the flock is black.
The black sheep that stood out from the ordinary run of sheep
  no longer stands out, for all the sheep are black.

Tá na prátaí dubh.
Tá na turnapaí dubh.
tá gach bileog cabáiste a chuirfeá síos i dtóin corcáin dubh.

Tá an sáspan dubh.
Tá an ciotal dubh.
Tá gach tóin corcáin as seo go Poll Tí Liabáin dubh.

Tá na Caitlicigh dubh.
Tá na Protastúnaigh dubh.
Tá na Seirbigh is na Cróátaigh dubh.
Tá gach uile chine a shiúlann ar dhromchla na cruinne
an mhaidin dhubh seo samhraidh, dubh.

Tá na polaiticeoirí ar sciobaidh
is iad ag baint na gcos is na n-eireaball dá chéile
ag iarraidh a chur ina luí orainn
nach fada go mbeidh gach dubh ina gheal.

Is an té a leomhadh a mhisneach dó
nó a chreidfeadh an méid a deireann siad
níor mhiste dó b'fhéidir an cheist a chur
ab ann ab amhlaidh a chiallaíonn sé seo anois
nach mbeidh ins gach dubhthréimhse ach seal?

The spuds are black.
The turnips are black.
Every last leaf of cabbage in the pot is black.

The saucepan is black.
The kettle is black.
The bottom of every pot from here to the crack of doom is
    black.

The Catholics are black.
The Protestants are black.
The Serbs and the Croatians are black.
Every tribe on the face of the earth this blackest of black
    mornings black.

The politicians are scuffling about
biting the legs and tails off each other
trying to persuade us
to look on the bright side.
Anyone who might be inclined
to take them at their word
would do well, maybe, to ask
why they think it goes without saying
that every black cloud has a silver lining.

Ach ní dhéanfadsa.
Mar táimse dubh.
Tá mo chroí dubh
is m'intinn dubh.
Tá m'amharc ar feadh raon mo radhairce dubh.
Tá an dubh istigh is amuigh agam díbh.

Mar gach píosa guail nó sméar nó airne,
gach deamhan nó diabhal nó daradaol,
gach cleite fiaigh mhara nó íochtar bhonn bróige,
gach uaimh nó cabha nó poll tóine
gach duibheagán doimhin a shlogann ár ndóchas,
táim dubh, dubh, dubh.

Mar tá Shrebrenice, cathair an airgid,
"Argentaria" na Laidne,
bán.

I myself won't be the one.
For I'm black.
My heart is black and my mind is black.
Everything that falls into my field of vision is black.
I'm full of black rage.
There's a black mark against all our names.

Like each and every lump of coal, every blackberry and sloe
and demon and devil and Devil's Coachman,
every grave and cave and arsehole,
every bottomless pit in which we lose all hope,
I'm black as black can be.

Now that Srebrenica, that silver city –
"Argentaria", as the Romans called it –
is blank.

BERNARD O'DONOGHUE

These poems are all linked to rural Ireland in various ways. "Caumatruish" is a townland just south of Millstreet, the town near which I grew up and where I went to secondary school. Dolly Duggan was a very close family friend, also from Millstreet (though she originated from Cork city), so the connection with those two poems is very direct. The nun was from the Aran Islands, as the poem says; but her experience was like that of girls – children, that is – I went to school with.

"The State of the Nation" is a bit different: it is a tribute to a wonderful television film made by an ex-student of mine, George Case, called *The Forgotten Holocaust*, about the appalling experiences of gipsies who disappeared in great numbers across Europe between 1935 and '45. The link is with the attitudes to Irish tinkers/travellers throughout my lifetime, which has left a lot to be desired; an attitude more recently extended to asylum-seekers. We of all peoples ought to welcome suffering immigrants.

"*Ter Conatus*" takes its title from a phrase in Virgil, referring to a motif also found in Homer, Dante and T.S. Eliot, in which a traveller from this world travels to the afterlife in bodily form. They encounter there the souls of people who had been dear to them in life; Aeneas meets his father Anchises and tries three times (. . . *ter conatus . . . Aeneid*, vi, 700) to embrace him, but his arms pass through him. He is, in Dante's phrase, "taking shadows for real things". And I am contrasting that myth with the common situation in farming Ireland in my childhood, when siblings often lived unmarried together through a long life, making very little physical contact with each other or anyone else: "taking real things for shadows", as the poem says.

I suppose what I would like to think is that these Irish situations have a universal quality to them: as Auden says, "like some valley cheese,/ local, but prized elsewhere".

A Nun Takes the Veil

That morning early I ran through briars
To catch the calves that were bound for market.
I stopped the once, to watch the sun
Rising over Doolin across the water.

The calves were tethered outside the house
While I had my breakfast: the last one at home
For forty years. I had what I wanted (they said
I could), so we'd loaf bread and Marie biscuits.

We strung the calves behind the boat,
Me keeping clear to protect my style:
Confirmation suit and my patent sandals.
But I trailed my fingers in the cool green water,

Watching the puffins driving homeward
To their nests on Aran. On the Galway mainland
I tiptoed clear of the cow-dunged slipway
And watched my brothers heaving the calves

As they lost their footing. We went in a trap,
Myself and my mother, and I said goodbye
To my father then. The last I saw of him
Was a hat and jacket and a salley stick,

Driving cattle to Ballyvaughan.
He died (they told me) in the county home,
Asking to see me. But that was later:
As we trotted on through the morning mist,

I saw a car for the first time ever,
Hardly seeing it before it vanished.
I couldn't believe it, and I stood up looking
To where I could hear its noise departing

But it was only a glimpse. That night in the convent
The sisters spoilt me, but I couldn't forget
The morning's vision, and I fell asleep
With the engine humming through the open window.

The State of the Nation

"The condition upon which God hath given liberty to man is
eternal vigilance" – JOHN PHILPOT CURRAN, 1790

Before I fell asleep, I had been reading
How in the Concentration Camps, alongside
The Jewish personal effects, were stored
For future reference gipsies' earrings,
Scarves and the crystal globes in which they saw
The future; and how the Guardia Civil
Swept through Fuente Vaqueros, smashing guitars.

The book was open still when I woke up
At dawn and, not reassured by the May chorus
From the cypresses, ran to the encampment
At the crossroads where slow smoke curled by the sign
"Temporary Dwellings Prohibited".
Still there; spread in dew along the hedges
Were gossamer and shawls and tea-towels.

A chained dog watched me peering under
The first canvas flap. Empty. The rest the same.
Not a soul in any tent. I straightened up
And listened through the sounds of morning
For voices raised in family rows, or their ponies
Tocking back from venial raids, bringing home
Hay, a clutch of eggs, unminded pullets.

Ter Conatus

Sister and brother, nearly sixty years
They'd farmed together, never touching once.
Of late she had been coping with a pain
In her back, realization dawning slowly
That it grew differently from the warm ache
That resulted periodically
From heaving churns on to the milking-stand.

She wondered about the doctor. When,
Finally, she went, it was too late,
Even for chemotherapy. And still
She wouldn't have got round to telling him,
Except that one night, watching television,
It got so bad she gasped, and struggled up,
Holding her waist. "D'you want a hand?", he asked,

Taking a step towards her. "I can manage",
She answered, feeling for the stairs.
Three times, like that, he tried to reach her.
But, being so little practised in such gestures,
Three times the hand fell back, and took its place,
Unmoving at his side. After the burial,
He let things take their course. The neighbours watched

Bernard O'Donoghue

In pity the rolled-up bales, standing
Silent in the fields, with the aftergrass
Growing into them, and wondered what he could
Be thinking of: which was that evening when,
Almost breaking with a lifetime of
Taking real things for shadows,
He might have embraced her with a brother's arms.

A Candle for Dolly Duggan
Venice, Easter 2001

Improbabilities of course, we all
know that: that this graceful taper
I force into the tallowed cast iron
beneath the *Assumption* in the Frari
could change the heavens, so that she
can pick up her cigarettes and lighter
to move on to a higher circle, as before
she moved, talking, through the lanes of Cork.

Sir Thomas Browne said there aren't impossibilities
enough in religion for an active faith.
So I'll go on spending liras and francs
and pesetas across the smoky hush
of Catholic Europe until she says
"That's enough", and then I'm free to toast
her in red wine outside in the sunlit squares.

The Iron Age Boat at Caumatruish

If you doubt, you can put your fingers
In the holes where the oar-pegs went.
If you doubt still, look past its deep mooring
To the mountains that enfold the corrie's
Waterfall of lace through which, they say,
You can see out but not in.
If you doubt that, hear the falcon
Crying down from Gneeves Bog
Cut from the mountain-top. And if you doubt
After all these witnesses, no boat
Dredged back from the dead
Could make you believe.

Cathal Ó Searchaigh

Last year, Suzy Conway, a very fine American poet, spent four or five months with me here in Mín 'a Leá, my homeplace. We are both Virgos but, unlike me, Suzy is fussily thorough in her Virgoism. She manifests orderliness, neatness, tidiness. She embodies these exacting traits. During her stay she got going on my house, and laid it out systematically; Vimmed and Harpicked and Windolened it into chaste spotlessness; put everything in alphabetical order, my books, my spices, even my emotions. She's a radical Virgo. Once I came back from Dublin to find out that all my curtains had been scrapped, completely done away with, abolished. The windows were bare as a newly born baby's backside. She said: "With curtains you have to ask yourself what are you trying to keep in or trying to keep out. Now the neighbours can see you properly." It's a new kind of kinky feminism. Get rid of your curtains and burn your blinds.

Suzy was of the opinion that poetry should not be pure but stark naked. Tonight, in my Suzyfied house with the moon, my mountainy neighbour, peeping in the window, I have fastidiously selected five poems that bare and reveal me (at least to myself and maybe to the moon).

I have an enduring trust in what Wordsworth called "the essential passions of the heart". "Serenade" is a poem that shimmers somewhere between the pagan eroticism of the *Táin Bó Cuailgne* and the lyrical charm of W.H. Auden's "Lullaby". I subscribe to the idea that the perfect love poem should be attuned to the five senses, the four elements and the seven deadly sins. And, like Martha Graham, I have "a queer divine dissatisfaction" with all that I write, coupled with "a blessed unrest" that keeps me "going, going, going".

Creativity for me arises, to a large extent, out of a deep attachment to my homeplace, a hillfarming, Gaelic-speaking community at the foot of Mount Errigal in North West Donegal. Like the Gaelic poets of my past I record and register what is past or passing in the locality. In this role I have become the collector, the archivist, the narrator of its memories and its myths. Poetry for me is a means of making memorable what is being forgotten, a way of gathering the past into the present, hoping that there will be a future for the past. "Lament" and "Here at Caiseal na nCorr Station" echo those concerns. What really fascinates people about rural Ireland, I think, is that here the past is always contemporary, an extended present you might say, which swings backwards and forwards effortlessly. Anyway, life as Nietzsche so aptly observed is lived forwards but understood backwards.

We all inhabit history, some people more than others of course. I think it is fair to say that the calamatious fate of millions is much easier to cope with than the tragic death of somebody that we know. Was it Stalin who said, "One million dead is a statistic, one dead individual is a tragedy"? Poems can be alert to politics, to the shadows cast by history, without being propaganda. "Postcard to Yusuf in Iraq" is my own feeble attempt to bear witness, to affirm the sovereignty of human love in a time of slaughter.

"Transfigured" is a poem about becoming a tree. I'm smitten by trees. I'm a tree hugger, a shrub cuddler. I sniff bark, taste resin, kiss leaves. I love to walk in woods, to breathe their leafy fragrance, to kneel down in their spirited presence. Somehow trees have taken root in my psyche. They swell and spread in my dreams. I'm a wood of whisperings. A leafy, shapeshifting Sweeney.

Laoi Chumainn

Anocht agus tú sínte síos le mo thaobh
a chaoin mhic an cheana, do chorp
teann téagartha, aoibh na hóige ort,
    anseo tá mé sábháilte
cuachta go docht faoi scáth d'uchta:
sleánna cosanta do sciathán
      mo chrioslú go dlúth
óir is tusa mo laoch, an curadh caol cruaidh
a sheasann idir mé agus uaigneas tíoránta na hoíche.

Is tusa mo laoch, mo thréan is mo neart,
mo Chú na gCleas agus níl fhios agam i gceart
cé acu an luan laoich é seo
    atá ag teacht ó do chneas
nó gríos gréine. Ach is cuma. Tá mé buíoch as an teas,
as na dealraitheacha deasa ó do ghrua
    a ghealaíonn mo dhorchadas,
as an dóigh a ndéanann tú an t-uaigneas
a dhiongbháil domh le fiochmhaireacht do ghrá.

Anocht má tá cath le fearadh agat, a ghrá,
bíodh sé anseo i measc na bpiliúr:
Craith do sciath agus gread do shleá,
    beartaigh do chlaíomh

Serenade

(translated by Frank Sewell)

Tonight, with you lying beside me,
my own darling boy, your body
taut and toned, glowing with youth,
    here I am safe,
tucked up tight in the shade of your chest,
your arms raised like spears to defend me,
    girding me firmly,
for you are my protection, my graceful bodyguard
who stands between me and the terror of lonely nights.

Yes, you are my hero, my tower of strength,
my Artful Hound, and I can't tell rightly
if it's valour shining
    around your skin
or the sun in heat. What difference? I'm glad
of the warmth, the fiery gleams of your cheeks
    that lighten my darkness,
glad of the way you fend off loneliness
with the sheer ferocity of love.

So, tonight, if there's a war to wage, my love,
let it be here among these pillows.
Raise your shield and hurl your lance,
    aim your sword

go beacht. Lig gáir churaidh as do bhráid.
Luífidh mé anseo ag baint sásamh súl
    as a bhfuil den fhear
ag bogadaigh ionat, a dhúil, go ndéanfaidh tú do bhealach féin
a bhearnú chugam fríd plúid agus piliúr.

Agus is toil liom, a mhacaoimh óig
gurb anseo ar léana mo leapa
a dhéanfá le barr feabhais
    do mhacghníomhartha macnais,
gurb anseo i ngleannta is i gcluanta
mo cholla, a thiocfá i dteann is i dtreise
    is go mbeadh gach ball
do mo bhallaibh, ag síorthabhairt grá duit
ar feadh síoraíocht na hoíche seo.

Anocht chead ag an domhan ciorclú
leis na beo is leis na mairbh:
Anseo i dtearmann dlúth na bpóg
    tá an saol ina stad:
Anseo i ndún daingean do bhaclainne
tá cúl ar chlaochlú. I bhfad uainn
    mairgí móra an tsaoil:
na tíortha is na treabha a dhéanfadh cocstí
de cheithre creasa na cruinne lena gcuid cogaíochta.

exactly. Get that war-cry off your chest.
And I will be here, all eyes
    at the manhood
moving in you, my passionate one, until you come
to meet me through sheets and pillows.

And, yes, it is my will, brave youth,
that on the field of my bed
you do your utmost
    to perform your manly deeds,
that here in the hills and hollows
of my flesh, you grow hard and strong
    as I give all
my all in limitless love to you
for the eternity of this night.

For, tonight, the world can beat about
with life and death.
Here, safe in the sanctuary of our kiss,
    time cannot catch up with us.
Tonight, in the fortitude of your arms,
we can be ourselves. The big bad world
    is far away
and we are free from countries and cunts
that would start a fight in an empty house.

Anocht, a mhacaoimh óig, bainimis fad saoil
as gach cogar, gach caoinamharc, gach cuimilt.
Amárach beidh muid gafa mar is gnáth
    i gcasadh cinniúnach na beatha,
i gcealg is i gcluain na Cinniúna.
Amárach díolfar fiacha na fola is na feola
    ach anocht, a fhir óig álainn,
tá muid i gciorcal draíochta an ghrá.
Ní bhuafaidh codladh orainn ná crá.

So, tonight, young man, let's make a life-time
of every whisper, glance or touch.
Tomorrow, we'll be back as usual,
          cogs in the wheel of fate,
pretending and conspiring with destiny.
Tomorrow, we'll pay for being flesh and blood;
          but tonight, my prince,
we are in the charmed circle of love.
No sleep or harm can defeat us.

Caoineadh

i gcuimhne mo mháthar

Chaoin mé na cuileatacha ar ucht mo mháthara
An lá a bhásaigh Mollie – peata de sheanchaora
Istigh i gcreagacha crochta na Beithí.
Á cuartú a bhí muid lá marbhánta samhraidh
Is brú anála orainn beirt ag dreasú na gcaorach
Siar ó na hailltreacha nuair a tchímid an marfach
Sna beanna dodhreaptha. Préacháin dhubha ina scaotha
Á hithe ina beatha gur imigh an dé deiridh aisti
De chnead choscrach amháin is gan ionainn iarraidh
Tharrthála a thabhairt uirthi thíos sna scealpacha.
Ní thiocfaí mé a shásamh is an tocht ag teacht tríom;
D'fháisc lena hucht mé is í ag cásamh mo chaill liom
Go dtí gur chuireas an racht adaí ó íochtar mo chroí.
D'iompair abhaile mé ansin ar a guailneacha
Ag gealladh go ndéanfadh sí ceapairí arán préataí.

Inniu tá mo theangaidh ag saothrú an bháis.
Ansacht na bhfilí – teangaidh ár n-aithreacha
Gafa i gcreagacha crochta na faillí
Is gan ionainn í a tharrtháil le dásacht.
Cluinim na smeachannaí deireanacha

Lament

in memory of my mother

(translated by Seamus Heaney)

I cried on my mother's breast, cried sore
The day Mollie died, our old pet ewe
Trapped on a rockface up at Beithí.
It was sultry heat, we'd been looking for her,
Sweating and panting, driving sheep back
From the cliff-edge when we saw her attacked
On a ledge far down. Crows and more crows
Were eating at her. We heard the cries
But couldn't get near. She was ripped to death
As we suffered her terrible, wild, last breath
And my child's heart broke. I couldn't be calmed
No matter how much she'd tighten her arms
And gather me close. I just cried on
Till she hushed me at last with a piggyback
And the promise of treats of potato-cake.

To-day it's my language that's in its throes,
The poets' passion, my mothers' fathers'
Mothers' language, abandoned and trapped
On a fatal ledge that we won't attempt.
She's in agony, I can hear her heave

Is na héanacha creiche ag teacht go tapaidh,
A ngoba craosacha réidh chun feille.
Ó dá ligfeadh sí liú amháin gaile – liú catha
A chuirfeadh na creachadóirí chun reatha,
Ach seo í ag creathnú, seo í ag géilleadh;
Níl mo mháthair anseo le mé a shuaimhniú a thuilleadh
Is ní dhéanfaidh gealladh an phian a mhaolú.

And gasp and struggle as they arrive,
The beaked and ravenous scavengers
Who are never far. Oh if only anger
Came howling wild out of her grief,
If only she'd bare the teeth of her love
And rout the pack. But she's giving in,
She's quivering badly, my mother's gone
And promises now won't ease the pain.

Anseo ag Stáisiún Chaiseal na gCorr

do Michael Davitt

Anseo ag Stáisiún Chaiseal na gCorr
d'aimsigh mise m'oileán rúin
mo thearmann is mo shanctóir.
Anseo braithim i dtiúin
le mo chinniúint féin is le mo thimpeallacht.
Anseo braithim seasmhacht
is mé ag feiceáil chríocha mo chineáil
thart faoi bhun an Eargail
mar a bhfuil siad ina gcónaí go ciúin
le breis agus trí chéad bliain
ar mhínte féaraigh an tsléibhe
ó Mhín an Leá go Mín na Craoibhe.
Anseo, foscailte os mo chomhair
go díreach mar bheadh leabhar ann
tá an taobh tíre seo anois
ó Dhoire Chonaire go Prochlais.
Thíos agus thuas tchím na gabháltais
a briseadh as béal an fhiántais.
Seo duanaire mo mhuintire;
an lámhscríbhinn a shaothraigh siad go teann
le dúch a gcuid allais.
Anseo tá achan chuibhreann mar bheadh rann ann
i mórdhán an mhíntíreachais.
Léim anois eipic seo na díograise
i gcanúint ghlas na ngabháltas

Here at Caiseal na gCorr Station

for Michael Davitt
(translated by Gabriel Fitzmaurice)

Here at Caiseal na gCorr Station
I discovered my hidden island,
my refuge, my sanctuary.
Here I find myself in tune
with my fate and environment.
Here I feel permanence
as I look at the territory of my people
around the foot of Errigal
where they've settled
for more than three hundred years
on the grassy mountain pastures
from Mín 'a Leá to Mín na Craoibhe.
Here before me, open
like a book,
is this countryside now
from Doire Chonaire to Prochlais.
Above and below, I see the holdings
farmed from the mouth of wilderness.
This is the poem-book of my people,
the manuscript they toiled at
with the ink of their sweat.
Here every enclosed field is like a verse
in the great poem of land reclamation.
I now read this epic of diligence
in the green dialect of the holdings,

is tuigim nach bhfuilim ach ag comhlíonadh dualgais
is mé ag tabhairt dhúshlán an fholúis
go díreach mar a thug mo dhaoine dúshlán an fhiántais
le dícheall agus le dúthracht
gur thuill siad an duais.

Anseo braithim go bhfuil éifeacht i bhfilíocht.
Braithim go bhfuil brí agus tábhacht liom mar dhuine
is mé ag feidhmiú mar chuisle de chroí mo chine
agus as an chinnteacht sin tig suaimhneas aigne.
Ceansaítear mo mhianta, séimhítear mo smaointe,
cealaítear contrárthachtaí ar an phointe.

understand that I'm only fulfilling my duty
when I challenge the void
exactly as my people challenged the wilderness
with diligence and devotion
till they earned their prize.

Here I feel the worth of poetry.
I feel my *raison d'être* and importance as a person
as I become the pulse of my people's heart
and from this certainty comes peace of mind.
My desires are tamed, my thoughts mellow,
contradictions are cancelled on the spot.

Cárta Poist chuig Yusuf san Iaráic

Anocht i mboige an Mhárta i Manhattan
Sheas mé ar leac dorais an tí
ina mbíodh cónaí ort i mBleeker Street
nuair a thug mé gean duit sna h-ochtóidí.

Mhoilligh mé ag doras úd an aoibhnis
ag cuimhniú ar oícheanta gealaí ár ngrá
nuair a bhíodh ár gcómhrá ar d'áit dhúchais –
mínte gréine na hIaráice idir Najaf agus Hillah.

Níl fhios agam cá bhfuil tú anocht
agus dúshraith an tsaoil ar crith, a chroí,
ó Najaf go Hillah; do dhaoine ag creathnú
roimh an neart gan cheart seo atá á n-ionsaí.

Tá buamaí na barbarthachta ag titim oraibh,
ag déanamh carnáin de bhur gcathracha, conamar de bhur
      mbailte,
agus is mór m'eagla go bhfuil do bheatha i mbaol
idir Najaf agus Hillah agus iad ag treascairt do thailte.

Anocht agus mé ag moilliú ag doras an tí úd
ag smaointiú ort, chuimhníos gur dhúirt tú liom tráth;
"Tá tír dhúchais an fhile le fáil i gcroíthe
na ndaoine atá faoi dhaorsmacht." Anocht, a ghrá

Postcard to Yusuf in Iraq
(translated by Frank Sewell)

"From the horizon of the individual to the horizon of humankind"
— Yevtushenko

Tonight, on a mild May evening in Manhattan
I stood on the front doorstep of the house
on Bleeker Street where you used to live
back in the early 80s when we were lovers.

I lingered long outside that doorway to heaven,
recalling night skies lit up with love
when we would talk of your homeland – the sunny plains
of Iraq between the cities of Hillah and Najaf.

Where you are tonight I do not know
as the world, my love, is shaken and awed
from Najaf to Hillah; your people terror-struck
by superpowers as wrong as they are strong.

Barbarian bombs are raining down on you,
turning your cities to ruins, your towns to rubble
as they raze your land from Hillah to Najaf
and heighten even more my fear for your life.

Tonight, caught in the shadow of your door,
I thought of you and what you said one time:
"The poet's place is in the heart of all
who are oppressed." All. Tonight, my love,

Caidé a thig liom a rá ach dearbhú duit
i dteangaidh bheag nach gcluintear sa challán
go bhfuil mé leat go h-iomlán. Tá an buama ag breith bua
ar mo bhriathra is an diúracán ag déanamh magaidh de mo dhán.

Ach anocht, tá mé leat, a fhir álann na hIaráice,
óir is é do chroíse amuigh ansiúd i mbéal an uafáis
fód beo mo dhúchais, fearann pinn mo dhaonnachta.
Dá bhrí sin, a mhian mo chroí is a dhíograis,

Dearbhaím go bhfuil mé leat anois ó bhaithis
mo chinn i Najaf go bonn mo choise i Hillah.

there is nothing I can do for you but pledge,
in a language unheard by the bigmouths,
that I am with you. Bombs are drowning out
my words, and bullets riddling my poem,

but tonight I am with you, Iraqi man,
because your heart, there in the teeth of terror,
is my land, the horizon of my humanity,
and that is why I say that I am with you,

brother, from the crown of my head in Najaf
down to the soles of my feet in Hillah.

Claochlú

Tá mé ag ullmhú le bheith i mo chrann
agus chan de bharr go bhfuil dia ar bith
'mo sheilg gan trua; é sa tóir orm go teann;
mé ag éalú óna chaithréim spéire, mo chroí ag rith
ina sceith sceoine, roimh bhuile a dhúile.

D'aonghnó tiocfaidh claochlú aoibhinn ar mo chló.
As mo cholainn daonna dhéanfar stoc darach.
Tiontóidh craiceann ina choirt chranrach; gan stró
athróidh an sruth fola ina shú, an gheir ina smúsach.
Fásfaidh duilleoga ar mo ghéaga cnámhacha.

Cheana féin tá mo chuid ladhra ag síneadh,
ag géagú amach ina bpréamhacha féitheogacha,
ag buanú sa chréafóg; ag taisceadh is ag teannadh.
Mothaím mé féin ag imeacht le craobhacha
nuair a shéideann bogleoithne fríd mo ghéaga.

Inniu chan ag análú atá mé ach ag siosarnach
agus mé mo sheasamh caol díreach gan bogadh;
éanacha na spéire ag ceiliúr ionam go haerach.
As an tsolas diamhair seo atá mo spreagadh
go dil, cruthóidh mé clóraifil, mo ghlasdán.

Transfigured
(translated by Frank Sewell)

I am getting ready to become a tree,
not because some god is after me,
bearing down with his aerial authority,
my heart bolting from the thrust of his need.

My figure will be transfigured, in one go;
my human shell turned to the trunk of an oak,
my skin twisted to gnarled bark, my blood flow
to sap. Out of my branch-bones leaves will grow.

Already, my fingers and toes are stretching out,
elongating into sinewy roots,
tucking themselves tightly into the ground;
and when a breeze blows my branches round,
I feel as if I'm going nuts, or out

of my tree. Today I stand tall and straight,
not breathing but rustling; birds congregate
in me, warbling airs while I create
chlorophyll, inspired by unfathomable light
to fulfil my destiny, synthesise my fate.

MICHEAL O'SIADHAIL

In choosing five poems to represent my work, I wanted poems that would stand alone, even though my books in later years have explored a particular theme. In *Love Life* I've written a whole book of love poems, but "Matins for You", from *Our Double Time*, anticipates all of them. "Loss" is a lament for my father-in-law – I think one of the hardest things is to share the grief of the person closest to us. "Courtesy" sums up some of what I find carries most meaning for me: poetry, music and painting; hospitality and friendship; and those moments when we can dare to celebrate our fragile city of trust. As for "Faces", perhaps the most enduring impression of the four years I spent immersed in Holocaust literature while writing *The Gossamer Wall* was imagining how each of the six million was a beloved face. My fifth choice is "Tremolo" from *Globe*. I find it almost unbearable to listen to the musics born out of the suffering of different peoples but the strange thing is how I hear some note of irrepressible hope crisscrossing our fragmented globe.

Matins for You

Come again glistening from your morning shower
Half-coquettishly you'll throw
Your robe at me calling out "Hello! Hello!"
I turn over stretching out to snatch
A bundle from the air and once more to watch
That parade across your bower.
Jaunty, brisk, allegro,
Preparing improvisations of yet another day,
As on our first morning twenty-seven years ago.

Sit on the bed-end and pull a stocking on,
Slip that frock over your head
Let it slither a little, ride your hips, then spread
Its folds and tumbles, flopping past those thighs
To swish against your ankles. I'm still all eyes.
The thrill and first frisson
At the half-known but unsaid,
At hints and contours embodied in a dance of dress
I'm ogling snugly from this your still warm bed.

Now you're hurrying, business-like and ready to go.
I wonder if I've ever glimpsed you
Or if all those years I even as much as knew
Behind those hints and suggestions I admire
What inmost aim or dream or heart's desire

Calls out "Hello, Hello!"
Flirt and peekaboo
Of such unwitting closeness, our take-for-grantedness,
Complex web of intimacies where we slowly grew.

Sometimes wells of aloneness seem almost to imbue
Your silence with the long wistful rubato
Of a Chopin nocturne or is it a *sean-nós* tremolo?
"Má bhíonn tú liom, bí liom, gach orlach de do chroí."
"If you're mine, be mine, each inch of your heart for me."
That infinite longing in you
A girl racing to follow
The bus's headlamps to meet your father at Bunbeg.
He steps down from the platform. Hello! Hello!

You smile your father's inward Zen-like smile.
And yet its light shines outward
As when I watched you helping a child to word
The coy, swaggering pleasure of new shoes,
A muse the more a muse in being a muse.
That inward outward smile
Delights in delight conferred,
Fine-tuning those strains and riffs of wishes unspoken,
Desires another's heart doesn't yet know it has heard.

Now I see you, now I don't. The doubt
And loneness of what's always new,
Moments seized in double time, love's impromptu,
As when late last night you started telling me
How even as a girl you'd known your dream would be
Bringing others' dreams about.
This once I think I glimpsed you,
You my glistening, lonely, giving Mistress Zen.
Thank you. Thank you for so many dreams come true.

Loss

The last summer he walked slower, chose to linger.
Pausing in a laneway, he ran a thumb along the seam of an old
    garden wall –
"Those joints need pointing" he warned; attentive, we saw in
    his face some strange
play of inward movement. On request we drove to Meath;
those fields a dozen times the size of his own
pleasured his eye. At Christmas leaning on the window sill,
Lovingly, he gazed over a few loamy acres towards Gola.
In mid January, cutting back briars, he fell with his scythe.

Several years later, I waken deep into the night,
hear you sobbing to yourself. It's Patrick's Eve,
That evening your father used return after
his winter exile, a labourer in Scotland; three
eager children watch the dark beyond Dunlewy.
Now, at last, the bus's headlamps arc the sky –
overjoyed you race the lights to meet him at Bunbeg.
Tonight, here by your side I listen, then kissing your forehead,
throw my arms around your sorrow.

Courtesy

1

I bring my basketful to serve
Our table. Everything mine is yours.
Everything. Without reserve.

Poems to which I still revert.
Gauguin. Matisse. Renoir's pear-shaped women.
Music I've heard. Blessed Schubert.

Ecstasies I'll never understand –
Mandelstam's instants of splendour, the world
A plain apple in his hand.

Lost faces. Those whose heirs
I was. My print-out of their genes,
Seed and breed of forbears.

Whatever I've become – courtesy
Of lovers, friends or friends of friends.
All those traces in me.

The living and dead. My sum
Of being. A host open and woundable.
Here I am!

2

Tiny as a firefly under the night sky,
We try to imagine stars that travel
Two million light years to reach the eye.

Long ago on a stormy and starless night
Old people used keep a half-door opened,
Anyone passing could make for the light.

The Russian astronauts leaving after them
Bread and salt for the next to dock
At the station. Small symbols of welcome.

Who's that outsider waiting for you?
We try to imagine how destinies unravel
Across the years towards their rendezvous.

A space for wanderers, lone or dispossessed.
At this table we've laid one empty place,
That old courtesy for the missing guest.

3

Never again just this.
Once-off. Ongoing wistfulness.
Wine loosening through my thighs.
Closeness. Our sudden huddle of intimacy.
These hours we're citizens of paradise.

A nourishment of senses.
Such fierce delight tenses
Between affections and the moments
When, like a theatre after its applause,
This house will fall again to silence.

Let gaieties outweigh
Their own misgivings. Emigré
And native, my desire attends
The moment in and out of time
Which even when it ceases never ends.

I feed on such courtesy.
These guests keep countenancing me.
Mine always mine. This complicity
Of faces, companions, breadbreakers.
You and you and you. My fragile city.

Faces

Neat millions of pairs of abandoned shoes
Creased with mute presence of those whose

Faces both stare and vanish. Which ghetto?
Warsaw, Vilna, Łódź, Riga, Kovno.

Eight hundred dark-eyed girls from Salonica
Bony and sag-breasted singing the *Hatikvah*

Tread the barefoot floor to a shower-room.
Friedlander, Berenstein, Menasche, Blum.

Each someone's fondled face. A named few.
Did they hold hands the moment they knew?

I'll change their shame to praise and renown in all
The earth . . . Always each face and shoeless footfall

A breathing memory behind the gossamer wall.

Tremolo

All that has been still an undertone,
Frets of memory half-heard deep
Below a hybrid croon of saxophone

Or when King Oliver's horn's darker
Notes warn a plantation child
He'd die an obscure poolroom marker.

A Bushman taps a hunting bow,
One end humming between the lips,
Drone of sound mesmeric and hollow.

At wedding gigs East Europe's blues
In moods of a harmonic minor scale
Blare a wistful klezmer rumpus.

Fingers strum a blown *mukkuri*
As swung against an Ainu's hips
A song of peace plucks a *tonkori*.

Once Turk or Khan, Rome or Greece,
Empires now where suns never fall,
A dominant bringing a dominant peace.

But one space of chosen nodes,
Mediant world of both/and plays
In flexitime, in different modes?

Given riffs and breaks of our own,
Given a globe of boundless jazz,
Yet still a remembered undertone,

A quivering earthy line of soul
Crying in all diminished chords.
Our globe still trembles on its pole.

BIOGRAPHIES

Eavan Boland was born in Dublin in 1944. Her collections of poetry include *23 Poems* (Gallagher, 1962), *The War Horse* (Gollancz, 1975), *In Her Own Image* (Arlen House, 1980), *Night Feed* (Arlen House, 1982), *The Journey* (Carcanet, 1987), *Selected Poems* (Carcanet, 1989), *Outside History* (Carcanet, 1990), *An Origin Like Water – Collected Poems* (New York, W.W. Norton, 1996), *Against Love Poetry* (W.W. Norton, 2003), *New Collected Poems* (Carcanet, 2005, and W.W. Norton, 2007) and *Domestic Violence* (Carcanet, and W.W. Norton, 2007).

Pat Boran was born in Portlaoise in 1963. His poetry collections include *The Unwound Clock* (Dedalus, 1990), *Familiar Things* (Dedalus, 1993), *The Shape of Water* (Dedalus, 1996), *As the Hand, the Glove* (Dedalus, 2001), and *New and Selected Poems* (Dedalus, 2007).

Ciaran Carson was born in Belfast in 1948. His poetry collections include *The New Estate* (Blackstaff Press, 1976), *The Irish for No* (The Gallery Press, 1987), *Belfast Confetti* (The Gallery Press, 1989), *First Language* (The Gallery Press, 1993), *Opera et Cetera* (The Gallery Press, 1996), *The Twelfth of Never* (London, Picador, 1999); *The Ballad of HMS Belfast* (The Gallery Press, 1999), *Breaking News* (The Gallery Press, 2003) and *For All We Know* (The Gallery Press, 2008).

Theo Dorgan was born in Cork in 1953. He is a member of Aosdána. His poetry collections include *The Ordinary House of Love* (Salmon Poetry, 1991), *Rosa Mundi* (Salmon Poetry, 1995), *Sappho's Daughter* (1998), *Songs of Earth and Light* (2005, translations from the Slovenian of Barbara Korun) and *What This Earth Cost Us* (Dedalus, 2008).

Paul Durcan was born in Dublin in 1944. His poetry collections include *Endsville* (with Brian Lynch) (New Writers' Press, 1967), *O Westport in the Light of Asia Minor* (Anna Livia Press, 1975), *Sam's Cross* (Profile Press, 1978), *Teresa's Bar* (The Gallery Press, 1976, revised edition, The Gallery Press, 1986), *Jesus, Break his Fall* (The Raven Arts Press, 1980), *Ark of the North* (Raven Arts Press, 1982), *The Selected Paul Durcan* (The Blackstaff Press, 1982), *Jumping the Train Tracks with Angela* (Raven Arts Press, 1983), *The Berlin Wall Café* (The Blackstaff Press, 1985), *Going Home to Russia* (The Blackstaff Press, 1987) , *In the Land of Punt* (with Gene Lambert) (Clashganna Mills Press, 1989), *Jesus and Angela* (The Blackstaff Press, 1998), *Daddy, Daddy* (The Blackstaff Press, 1990), *Crazy About Women* (The National Gallery of Ireland, 1991), *A Snail in My Prime: New and Selected Poems* (The Harvill Press, 1993), *Give Me Your Hand* (Macmillan, in association with National Gallery Publications, 1994), *Christmas Day* (The Harvill Press, 1997), *Greetings to Our Friends in Brazil* (The Harvill Press, 1999), *Cries of an Irish Caveman* (The Harvill Press, 2001), *The Art of Life* (The Harvill Press, 2004) and *The Laughter of Mothers* (Harvill Secker, 2007).

Peter Fallon was born in 1951. His poetry collections include *Eye To Eye* (The Gallery Press, 1992), *News of the World: Selected and New Poems* (The Gallery Press, 1998), *The Georgics of Virgil* (The Gallery Press, 2004, and

Oxford World's Classics, 2006) and *The Company of Horses* (The Gallery Press, 2007).

Kerry Hardie was born in Singapore in 1951, and grew up in County Down. Her poetry collections include *A Furious Place* (The Gallery Press, 1996), *Cry for the Hot Belly* (The Gallery Press, 2000), *The Sky Didn't Fall* (The Gallery Press, 2003) and *The Silence Came Close* (The Gallery Press, 2006).

Seamus Heaney was born in Co. Derry in 1939. He won the 1995 Nobel Prize for Literature. His poetry collections include *Death of a Naturalist* (Faber and Faber, 1966), *Door Into the Dark* (Faber and Faber, 1969), *Wintering Out* (Faber and Faber, 1972), *North* (Faber and Faber, 1975); *Field Work* (Faber and Faber, 1979), *Selected Poems, 1965–1975* (Faber and Faber, 1980), *Poems, 1965–1975* (Farrar, Straus, and Giroux, 1980), *Station Island* (Faber and Faber, 1984), *The Haw Lantern* (Farrar, Straus, and Giroux, 1987), *New Selected Poems, 1966–1987* (Faber and Faber, 1990), *Seeing Things* (Farrar, Straus, and Giroux, 1991), *The Spirit Level* (Faber and Faber, 1996), *Opened Ground: Poems, 1966–1996* (Faber and Faber, 1998), *Electric Light* (Faber, 2001) and *District and Circle* (Faber and Faber, 2006).

Rita Ann Higgins was born in Galway. She has published eight collections of poetry, five with Salmon Publishing and three with Bloodaxe, including her latest collection *Throw in the Vowels: New and Selected Poems* (2005). Her most recent plays include *The Big Break* (screenplay, 2004), *The Empty Frame* (a play for stage inspired by Hanna Greally) (2008) and *The Plastic Bag* (2008), a play for radio. She was

Green Honors Professor at TCU in 2000 and an honorary fellow at HKB University in 2006. Other awards include a Peadar O'Donnell award and several Arts Council bursaries. *Sunny Side Plucked* was a poetry book society recommendation. She has been writer-in-residence at the National University of Ireland. She is a member of Aosdána.

Brendan Kennelly was born in Ballylongford, Co. Kerry, in 1936. His poetry collections include *Cast a Cold Eye* (with Rudi Holzapfel) (Dolmen Press, 1959), *The Rain, the Moon* (with Rudi Holzapfel) (Dolmen Press, 1961), *The Dark About Our Loves* (John Augustine and Co.,1962), *Green Townlands* (Leeds University Bibliography Press, 1963), *Let Fall No Burning Leaf* (New Square Publications, 1963), *My Dark Fathers* (New Square, 1964), *Up and At It* (New Square, 1965), *Collection One: Getting Up Early* (Allen Figgis, 1966), *Good Souls to Survive* (Allen Figgis, 1967), *Dream of a Black Fox* (Allen Figgis, 1968), *Selected Poems* (Allen Figgis, 1969), *A Drinking Cup, Poems from the Irish* (Allen Figgis, 1970), *Bread* (Tara Telephone Publications, 1971), *Love Cry* (Allen Figgis, 1972), *Salvation, The Stranger* (Tara Telephone Publications, 1972); *The Voices* (The Gallery Press, 1973), *Shelley in Dublin* (Anna Livia Press), *A Kind of Trust* (The Gallery Press, 1975), *New and Selected Poems* (The Gallery Press, 1976), *Islandman* (Profile Press, 1977), *The Visitor* (St Beuno's Press, 1978), *A Small Light* (The Gallery Press, 1979), *In Spite of the Wise* (Trinity Closet Press, 1979), *The Boats Are Home* (The Gallery Press, 1980), *The House That Jack Didn't Build* (Beaver Row Press, 1982), *Cromwell* (Beaver Row Press, 1983), *Moloney Up and At It* (The Mercier Press, 1984), *Selected Poems* (Kerrymount Publications, 1985), *Mary* (Aisling, 1987), *Love of Ireland: Poems from the Irish* (Mercier Press, 1989), *A Time for Voices: Selected Poems 1960–1990* (Bloodaxe Books, 1990), *The*

Book of Judas (Bloodaxe Books, 1991), *Poetry My Arse* (Bloodaxe Books, 1995), *The Man Made of Rain* (Bloodaxe Books, 1998), *The Singing Tree* (Abbey Press, 1998), *Glimpses* (Bloodaxe Books, 2001), *The Little Book of Judas* (Bloodaxe Books, 2003), *Martial Art* (Bloodaxe Books, 2003), *Familiar Strangers: New and Selected Poems 1960–2004* (Bloodaxe Books, 2004) and *Now* (Bloodaxe Books, 2006).

Michael Longley was born in Belfast in 1939, and educated at The Royal Belfast Academical Institution and Trinity College, Dublin, where he read Classics. He has published eight collections of poetry including *Gorse Fires* (1991) which won the Whitbread Award, and *The Weather in Japan* (2000) which won the Hawthornden Prize, the T.S. Eliot Prize and the *Irish Times* Poetry Prize. His most recent collection, *Snow Water* (2004), was awarded the Librex Montale Prize. In 2001 he received the Queen's Gold Medal for Poetry, and in 2003 the Wilfred Owen Award. He and his wife, the critic Edna Longley, live and work in Belfast.

Derek Mahon was born in Belfast in 1941. His poetry collections include *Night-Crossing* (Oxford University Press, 1968), *Lives* (Oxford University Press, 1972), *The Snow Party* (Oxford University Press, 1975), *Poems 1962–1978* (Oxford University Press, 1979), *Courtyards in Delft* (Oxford University Press, 1981), *The Hunt By Night* (Oxford University Press, 1982), *Antarctica* (The Gallery Press, 1985), *Selected Poems* (The Gallery Press, 1990), *The Hudson Letter* (The Gallery Press, 1995), *The Yaddo Letter* (The Gallery Press, 1992), *The Yellow Book* (The Gallery Press, 1997), *Collected Poems* (The Gallery Press, 1999), *Harbour Lights* (The Gallery Press, 2005) and *Homage to Gaia* (The Gallery Press, 2008).

Medbh McGuckian was born in Belfast in 1950. Her poetry collections include *The Flower Master* (Oxford University Press, 1982), *Venus and the Rain* (Oxford University Press, 1984), *On Ballycastle Beach* (Oxford University Press, 1988), *Marconi's Cottage* (The Gallery Press, 1991), *Captain Lavender* (The Gallery Press, 1994), *Selected Poems* (The Gallery Press, 1997), *Drawing Ballerinas* (The Gallery Press, 2001), *The Face of the Earth* (The Gallery Press, 2002), *Had I a Thousand Lives* (The Gallery Press, 2003), *The Book of the Angel* (The Gallery Press, 2004) and *The Currach Requires No Harbours* (The Gallery Press, 2006).

Paula Meehan was born in Dublin in 1955. Her poetry collections include *Return and No Blame* (Beaver Row Press, 1984), *Reading the Sky* (Beaver Row Press, 1986), *The Man Who was Marked by Winter* (The Gallery Press, 1991), *Pillow Talk* (The Gallery Press, 1994), *Mysteries of the Home: A Selection of Poems* (Bloodaxe Books, 1996), *Dharmakaya* (Carcanet Press, 2000), and, forthcoming in 2009, *Painting Rain* (Carcanet Press).

John Montague was born in Brooklyn, New York, in 1929. His poetry collections include *Forms of Exile* (Dolmen Press, 1958), *Poisoned Lands* (Dolmen Press, 1961), *A Chosen Light* (Macgibbon and Kee, 1967), *Tides* (Dolmen Press, 1971), *The Rough Field* (Dolmen, 1972), *A Slow Dance* (Dolmen, 1975), *The Great Cloak* (Dolmen, 1978), *The Dead Kingdom* (Dolmen, 1984), *Mount Eagle* (The Gallery Press, 1989), *The Love Poems* (Exile Editions, 1992), *Time in Armagh* (The Gallery Press, 1993), *Collected Poems* (The Gallery Press, 1995), *Smashing the Piano* (The Gallery Press, 1999) and *Drunken Sailor* (The Gallery Press, 2004).

Sinéad Morrissey was born in Portadown, Northern Ireland, in 1972. Her poetry collections include *There Was Fire in Vancouver* (Carcanet

Press, 1996), *Between Here and There* (Carcanet, 2002), and *The State of the Prisons* (Carcanet, 2005). She was the recipient of the Patrick Kavanagh Award in 1990; an Eric Gregory Award in 1996; the Rupert and Eithne Strong Award in 2002; and the Michael Hartnett Poetry Prize in 2005. *Between Here and There* and *The State of the Prisons* were both shortlisted for the T.S. Eliot Prize. In 2007 she received a Lannan Literary Fellowship and was the winner of the UK's National Poetry Competition with the poem, "Through the Square Window". She is lecturer in Creative Writing at the Seamus Heaney Centre for Poetry, Queen's University, Belfast.

Nuala Ní Dhomhnaill was born in Lancashire in 1952. Her poetry collections include *An Dealg Droighin* (Mercier Press, 1981), *Féar Suaithinseach* (An Sagart, 1984), *Rogha Dánta/Selected Poems* (translated by Michael Hartnett) (Raven Arts Press, 1986), *Pharoah's Daughter* (The Gallery Press, 1990), *Feis* (An Sagart, 1991), *Cead Aighnis* (An Sagart, 1999), *The Water Horse* (The Gallery Press, 1999), *The Astrakhan Cloak* (The Gallery Press, 2001) and *The Fifty Minute Mermaid* (The Gallery Press, 2007).

Bernard O'Donoghue was born in Co Cork in 1945. His poetry books include *The Weakness* (Chatto & Windus, 1992), *Gunpowder* (Chatto & Windus, 1995), *Here Nor There* (Chatto & Windus, 1999), *Poaching Rights* (The Gallery Press, 1999) and *Outliving* (Chatto & Windus, 2003).

Cathal Ó Searchaigh was born in Donegal in 1956. He is a member of Aosdána. His collections of poetry include *Homecoming/An Bealach 'na Bhaile* (Cló Iar-Chonnachta, 1993), *Na Buachaillí Bána* (Cló Iar-Chonnachta, 1995) and *An Tnúth leis an tSolas* (Cló Iar-Chonnachta, 2001), *Gúrú i gCluidíní* (Cló Iar-Chonnachta, 2006).

Micheal O'Siadhail was born in Dublin in 1947. His collections are *The Leap Year* (An Clóchomhar, 1978), *Rungs of Time* (An Clóchomhar, 1980), *Belonging* (An Clóchomhar, 1982), *Springnight* (Bluett, 1983), *The Image Wheel* (Bluett, 1985), *The Chosen Garden* (Dedalus, 1990), *Hail! Madam Jazz: New and Selected Poems* which includes *The Middle Voice* (Bloodaxe Books, 1992), *A Fragile City* (Bloodaxe Books, 1995), *Our Double Time* (Bloodaxe Books, 1998), *Poems 1975–1995* (Bloodaxe Books, 1999), *The Gossamer Wall: Poems in Witness to the Holocaust* (Bloodaxe Books, 2002), *Love Life* (Bloodaxe Books, 2005) and *Globe* (Bloodaxe 2007).

COPYRIGHT ACKNOWLEDGEMENTS

The editor gratefully acknowledges the permission of individuals and publishers to reprint the following copyrighted material:

Eavan Boland and the Carcanet Press for "Atlantis: A Lost Sonnet" from *Domestic Violence*, "A Woman Painted on a Leaf" from *In a Time of Violence*, "How the Dance Came to the City" from *Domestic Violence*, "The Emigrant Irish" from *The Journey* and "Love" from *In a Time of Violence*.

Pat Boran and the Dedalus Press for "Children", "Waving" and "Seven Unpopular Things to Say about Blood" from *Familiar Things*, "Machines" and "The Washing of Feet" from *As the Hand, the Glove*.

Ciaran Carson and The Gallery Press for "The Bomb Disposal", "Dresden", "Second Language", "Gallipoli" from "The War Correspondent", and "The Shadow", all from *Collected Poems*.

Theo Dorgan and the Dedalus Press for "Kilmainham Gaol, Dublin, Easter 1991", "Seven Versions of Loss Eternal" and "Thornship" from *What The Earth Cost Us* and Theo Dorgan for "On A Day Far From Now" and "Ithaca".

Paul Durcan for "The Death by Heroin of Sid Vicious" from *Jesus, Break His Fall*, "'Windfall', 8 Parnell Hill, Cork" from *The Berlin Wall Café*, "Diarrhoea Attack at Party Headquarters In Leningrad" from *Going Home To Russia*, "Our Father" from *Daddy, Daddy* and "Rosie Joyce" from *The Art of Life*.

Peter Fallon and The Gallery Press for "Go", "The Company of Horses" and "The Less Ado" from *The Company of Horses*, "Gate" from *News of the World: New and Selected Poems*, and Peter Fallon for "After the Storm".

Kerry Hardie and The Gallery Press for "Avatar" from *A Furious Place*, "Exiles" from *Cry for the Hot Belly*, "When Maura Had Died" from *The Sky Didn't Fall*, "Derrynane '05" and "The High Pyrenees" from *The Silence Came Close*.

Seamus Heaney and Faber and Faber for "The Tollund Man" from *Wintering Out*, "Casualty" and "The Harvest Bow" from *Field Work*, "A Sofa in the Forties" from *The Spirit Level* and "The Blackbird of Glanmore" from *District and Circle*.

Rita Ann Higgins for "Ciontach" ("Guilty"), "The Immortals", "Dirty Dancer", "The Darkness" and "Borders".

Brendan Kennelly and Bloodaxe Books for "God's Eye", "Eily Kilbride", "Poem from a Three Year Old", "Yes" and "Begin", all from *Familiar Strangers: New and Selected Poems 1960–2004*.

Michael Longley and Cape Poetry for "The Linen Industry" from *The Echo Gate*, "Ceasefire" from *The Ghost Orchid*, "Ghetto" from *Gorse Fires*, "Etruria" from *The Weather in Japan* and "The Leveret" from *Collected Poems*.

Derek Mahon and The Gallery Press for "An Unborn Child", "A Disused Shed in Co. Wexford", "A Garage in Co. Cork", "Shapes and Shadows" and "Roman Script", all from *Collected Poems*.

Medbh McGuckian and The Gallery Press for "Waters" from *Venus and the Rain*, "Yeastlight" from *On Ballycastle Beach*, "White Magpie" from *Shelmalier*, "Turning the Moon into a Verb" from *Marconi's Cottage* and "Viewing Neptune Through a Glass Telescope" from *The Face of the Earth*.

Paula Meehan and The Gallery Press for "Well" from *The Man Who Was Marked by Winter* and "Home" from *Pillow Talk*; Paula Meehan and Carcanet Press for "On Poetry" from *Dharmakaya*, and Paula Meehan for "Death of a Field" and "Quitting the Bars".

John Montague and The Gallery Press for "Courtyard in Winter", "A Flowering Absence", "Herbert Street Revisited" and "Mount Eagle" from *Collected Poems*, and "Last Court" from *Drunken Sailor*.

Sinéad Morrissey for "Storm", "Apocrypha", "Found Architecture", "Love, the Nightwatch . . ." and "Through the Square Window".

Nuala Ní Dhomhnaill, Paul Muldoon and The Gallery Press for "An Crann" ("As for the Quince") and "An Bhean Mhídhílis" ("The Unfaithful Wife") from *Pharaoh's Daughter* and "Dubh" ("Black") from *The Fifty Minute Mermaid*; Nuala Ní Dhomnaill and New Island Books for "Leaba Shíoda" and "Máthair" from *Selected Poems: Rogha Dánta*.

Bernard O'Donoghue for "A Nun Takes the Veil" and "The State of the Nation" from *The Weakness*, "*Ter Conatus*" from *Here Nor There*, "A Candle for Dolly Duggan" from *Outliving* and "The Iron Age Boat at Caumatruish" from *Gunpowder*.

Cathal Ó Searchaigh for "Laoi Chumainn" ("Serenade"), "Caoineadh" ("Lament") and "Anseo ag Stáisiún Chaiseal na gCorr" ("Here at Caiseal na gCorr Station") from *Homecoming – An Bealach 'na Bhaile* (Cló Iar-Chonnachta, 1993), "Cárta Poist chuig Yusuf san Iaráic" ("Postcard to Yusuf in Iraq") from *Gúrú i gClúidíní* (Cló Iar-Chonnachta, 2006) and "Claochlú" ("Transfigured") from *Ag Tnúth Leis an tSolais* (Cló Iar-Chonnachta, 2000).

Micheal O'Siadhail and Bloodaxe Books for "Matins for You" from *Our Double Time*, "Loss" from *The Image Wheel*, "Faces" from *The Gossamer Wall*, "Tremolo" from *Globe* and "Courtesy" from *A Fragile City*.